The Compact Guide to the
Bible

The Compact Guide to the
Bible

LION

Debra K. Reid
Martin Manser

Copyright © 2010 Debra K. Reid and Martin Manser
This edition copyright © 2010 Lion Hudson

The authors assert the moral right
to be identified as the authors of this work

A Lion Book
an imprint of
Lion Hudson plc
Wilkinson House, Jordan Hill Road,
Oxford OX2 8DR, England
www.lionhudson.com

ISBN 978 0 7459 5313 7

Distributed by:
UK: Marston Book Services, PO Box 269, Abingdon, Oxon, OX14 4YN
USA: Trafalgar Square Publishing, 814 N. Franklin Street, Chicago, Illinois 60610
USA Christian Market: Kregel Publications, PO Box 2607, Grand Rapids, Michigan 49501

First edition 2010
10 9 8 7 6 5 4 3 2 1 0

Acknowledgments
Scripture quotations taken from the Holy Bible, *Today's New International Version*. Copyright ©
2004 by International Bible Society. Used by permission of Hodder & Stoughton Publishers. A
member of the Hachette Livre UK Group. All rights reserved. 'TNIV' is a registered trademark of
International Bible Society.
p. 169: Scripture taken from the New American Standard Bible, Copyright © 1960,1962, 1963,
1968,1971,1972,1973,1975,1977,1995 by The Lockman Foundation. Used by permission.
The authors are grateful to HarperCollins for giving their permission to publish extracts from
Dictionary of the Bible (ed. Martin Selman and Martin Manser), to Facts on File for giving their
permission to publish extracts from *Critical Companion to the Bible* (ed. Martin Manser), and to
IVP and InterVarsity Press USA for giving their permission to publish an extract from *Tyndale
New Testament Commentary, John* (by Colin G. Kruse).

The authors are also grateful to our commissioning editors Kate Kirkpatrick, Stephanie Heald
and Morag Reeve for their guidance and encouragement.

A catalogue record for this book is available from the British Library.

Typeset in 9.5/11 Bodoni Svty Two ITC TT
Printed and bound in China

Websites:
www.spurgeons.ac.uk and www.martinmanser.com

Contents

Introduction

Life is a journey. Like all journeys, it has its moments of questioning, adventure and exploration. We can ask many questions about the Bible: Where did the Bible come from? Who wrote it? Who was Abraham? Where is Nineveh? What was the purpose of the Ark of the Covenant? We've written this book to be a reliable guide to answering such questions. There are much longer books that give you fuller answers (and we've listed some of these at the ends of chapters), but this book gives you a clear, reliable overview of the background to the Bible.

As you explore the Bible, you may find yourself asking some more personal questions: What does it mean to have Christian faith? How can I apply the Bible to life today? We suggest that as you read this book, you actually read it alongside the Bible itself. In this way, we hope you will begin to understand the message of the Bible... and that is the adventure of a lifetime.

Debra K. Reid

Martin Manser

1

What is the Bible?

More than a collection of writings

Christians consider the Bible to be the most important book that has ever been compiled. It has been translated into more languages and has sold more copies than any other book that has ever been written and published. However, the apparently simple question, 'What is the Bible?' is a very difficult one to answer. In fact, there are as many ways to answer this question as there are reasons for asking it.

The general purpose of this book is to provide some response to this question for those seeking to understand more about the Bible. But understanding the Bible better is not the same as being able to define what the Bible actually *is*. Consider these statements about the Bible:

◆ 'The Bible is a collection of writings written over a long period of time which came to be recognized by the church as scripture.' *This statement defines the Bible in terms of how it came into being: it is concerned with the Bible's origins.*

◆ 'The Bible is a label given to the Christian scriptures, consisting of the Old and New Testaments.' *This statement is concerned with the content of the Bible.*

◆ '[The Bible is] the most valuable thing that this world affords... Here is wisdom; this is the royal law; these are the lively oracles of God.'[1] *This third statement is more about the status and value of the Bible.*

The first two statements are commonly reflected in standard English dictionaries because they are universally accepted answers to questions about how the term 'Bible' is used in the English language. The third offers more than this: it is a statement that reflects the faith that generations of Christians have placed in the Bible. The mention of faith in the Bible is significant

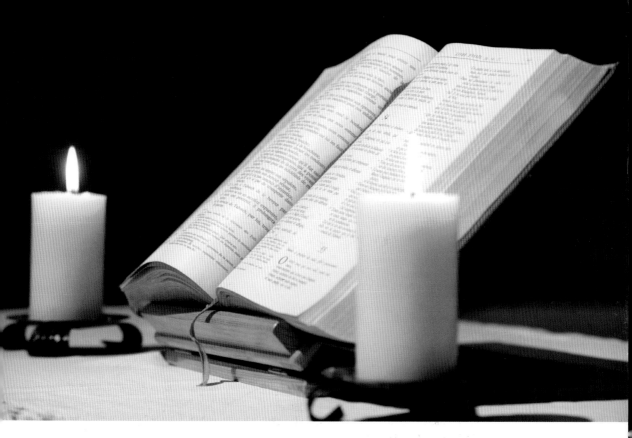

because the Bible is a collection of books that were written as testimonies to a faith that has developed over many centuries. These books record a journey of faith with the aim of inspiring faith. It is this faith on which the third statement relies.

Life in biblical times

This introduction to the Bible contains some information about the cultural and historical aspects of life during biblical times. But insights into the religion and faith of the people that the Bible introduces are also included. History and faith are intertwined in the Bible just as personal, national and international history is intertwined with the faith or non-faith upon which lives, societies and national identities are based.

An explanation of terms:

Scriptures means 'writings'
Testament means 'will' or 'covenant' or 'witness'

The word 'Bible'

The English word 'Bible' comes from the Latin *biblia*, which in turn comes from a Greek word that means 'books', recognizing the fact that the Bible is a collection, or library. In fact, most copies of the Bible today are divided into sixty-six books. There are thirty-nine books in the first part of this library, known as the Old Testament, and twenty-seven books in the second part, known as the New Testament. Additional books are included in some Bible editions (see chapter 1, **The Apocrypha**).

The authority of the Bible

The Bible is known by a variety of names: *the Holy Bible, the Holy Scriptures, Scripture, the word of God*. These terms emphasize the way in which Christian people have given the Bible a special status and authority. This fact is so widely recognized that the word 'bible' has come to be used to refer to all kinds of resources that have been given a special status among others, so a 'bible' of French cooking and a 'bible' of car maintenance are available. A 'bible' stands apart from other ordinary resources as being different. It is *the* authority and not just *an* authority. Christians assert more, however: they claim that the Bible is uniquely authoritative because it is relevant not in just one sphere of life but across all spheres of life.

The Bible has its own history. The rest of this chapter will look at three important aspects of that history: the languages in which it was written, the way in which the text of the Bible has been transmitted, and the process by which its present contents were selected.

The languages of the Bible

The Bible was written in three languages: Classical Hebrew, Biblical Aramaic (or Chaldee) and Koine (Common) Greek.

Most of the Old Testament is written in Hebrew, although a few Aramaic texts occur. The New Testament is written in Koine Greek although occasional Aramaic words appear – not surprisingly, as Aramaic was the language that Jesus and his Jewish contemporaries would have spoken.

Classical Hebrew

Classical Hebrew belongs to the group of languages known as the 'Classical Semitic languages' (that is, Hebrew, Syriac, Geez, Aramaic and Akkadian). This was the predominant language group in the Near East in Old Testament times. Classical Hebrew became the language of the Jews once they entered Canaan, and the Hebrew biblical texts suggest that the language remained remarkably consistent despite the wide geographical, cultural and historical spread of these texts. It would not be true to say that the Hebrew of the Old Testament is consistent in every aspect, but the writers keep to a defined language system with a single grammatical framework.

Originally the Old Testament text was written in words that contained only consonants. It wasn't until the time of the Masoretes (AD 600–900) that the vowels and the punctuation system found in present editions of the Hebrew Old Testament were added.

Biblical Aramaic (Chaldee)

As the Assyrians (see chapter 7) rose to power they developed Aramaic as the common language of their empire, and it achieved widespread use in the Near East (see chapter 2 where this term is explained more fully). First the neo-Babylonian empire (605–539 BC) and then the Persian empire after its conquest of Babylon (539–330 BC) continued this process (see chapter 2, **Historical setting**). As Aramaic became the *lingua franca* of the Persian empire, a formal Aramaic style was adopted for official and legal documents. This formal Aramaic was influenced by various spoken dialects resulting in the type of written Aramaic that we find in the Aramaic portions of the Old Testament. Aramaic only accounts for a very small proportion of the Old Testament text: passages in Daniel 2–7, and Ezra 4–6 and 7, and a single verse in Jeremiah (10:11). The changes from Hebrew to Aramaic (and back again) in both Ezra and Daniel suggest that the writers of these Old Testament texts were proficient in both languages. The form of Aramaic that is used in these texts was used by Jews for a long time and lasted at least into the Middle Ages. However, the popularity of the Aramaic language obviously faded as the Greek empire advanced.

Although the New Testament is written in Greek, Jesus and the Jews of his time would have used Aramaic as their main language. For this reason we see some clear examples of Aramaic influences on the text of the New Testament both in terms of words used and style adopted.

Koine Greek

Although the people in the New Testament would also have spoken Aramaic and Latin, it is the language of the Greek empire that became the primary medium for recording the events of Jesus' lifetime and their immediate aftermath.

The Greek language had spread rapidly in the Near East since Alexander's conquests (334–324 BC) – even though the Maccabean uprising (see glossary)

An extract from the 'Psalms scroll' from Qumran, near the Dead Sea, showing Hebrew script and dating from c. AD 30–50.

Content of the main Aramaic passages in the Old Testament

Daniel (2:4 – 7:28)
◆ speech of the astrologers (Chaldeans) to King Nebuchadnezzar;
◆ further narrative;
◆ conversation with the king;
◆ the king's decrees and his dreams;
◆ Daniel's role as interpreter;
◆ Daniel's own dream.

This section of the book of Daniel is set in the Persian royal court.

Ezra (Ezra 4:8 – 6:18; 7:12–26)
◆ letters to and from Darius, the Persian king;
◆ royal decrees of Darius;
◆ Artaxerxes' letter to Ezra.

Examples of Aramaic words used in the New Testament

Matthew 5:22 *raca* (meaning 'worthless fool': a term of contempt)

Matthew 16:17 *Simon bar Jonah* (bar is Aramaic for 'son')

Matthew 27:46 and Mark 15:34 *Eli, Eli lama sabachthani* (meaning 'My God, my God, why have you forsaken me?'), quoted from Psalm 22, but here sabachthani is in Aramaic form

Mark 5:41 *talitha cumi* (meaning 'Little girl, get up!')

Mark 7:34 *ephphratha* (meaning 'be opened')

Mark 10:51 *rabboni* (meaning 'my teacher/Rabbi')

Mark 14:26 *abba* (meaning 'father', also Romans 8:15; Galatians 4:6)

1 Corinthians 16:22 *maranatha* (meaning 'come, Lord')

meant that Hebrew was placed alongside it, albeit temporarily, as an official language in Jerusalem. The popularity of Greek philosophy helped to make sure that Greek held its ground, even when the Romans brought the Latin language with them, because it was so strongly rooted as the language of education and learning in both Hellenistic and Jewish circles. For Jewish people spread throughout the region it was essential to be able to communicate with the people around them, and increasingly Koine Greek became the language of everyday life in Jewish homes too. So Koine Greek provided the possibility for communication with the whole Greco-Roman world, something the Gospel writers, and other New Testament writers, were of course eager to do (see Luke 1:3).

The New Testament writers also chose to use the Greek Septuagint (see glossary) as their source when they included Old Testament quotations in their writings. This means that we can be relatively sure that this Greek version of the Old Testament had already secured a firm place as the scripture generally used in the early church. Despite this incorporation of Greek influences, there are many examples of how the Jewishness of the New Testament writers has left its mark on the Greek New Testament text. For example, Hebrew and Aramaic sentence structure is common rather than a pure Greek style. The result is that the Greek of the New Testament is quite distinct from that found in contemporary texts from other origins.

The transmission of the Bible

Although Christians believe that God inspired the text of the Bible, the task of writing, preserving, circulating and translating the Bible was entrusted to a variety of human hands. This task was often difficult, but the story of the transmission of the Bible bears witness to the seriousness with which people approached it.

The transmission of the Old Testament

Although there are many manuscripts of Old Testament texts, we have none older than those that were found in a cave overlooking the Dead Sea in a place called Qumran (see chapter 2, **Dead Sea scrolls** and chapter 7, **Essenes**).

These manuscripts, preserved by a devoutly religious Jewish group, date from between 250 and 150 BC. The initial discovery was made in 1946, but it took some years to uncover the many scrolls that are now available to scholars. The very fact that the Old Testament had been preserved for so many years between the writing of the individual books and the date of the Qumran manuscripts, indicates the central place the Old Testament books assumed in Jewish communities in these intervening years. During this time Jewish scribes and scholars faithfully copied Old Testament texts and handed them down from one generation to the next. Their dual aim seems to have been to preserve the text faithfully and to ensure that it was understood in their own day. By the start of the first century AD a third aim

Far left: A papyrus document written in Aramaic, dated 449 BC. Referring to freedom from slavery, it was found on Elephantine Island, Egypt.

Above: Detail of a floor mosaic originally located in the House of the Faun, Pompeii. The detail depicts Alexander the Great at the Battle of Issus against Darius III in 333 BC.

Left: The Codex Sinaiticus is a 4th-century manuscript of the Greek Bible, written between AD 330–350.

The names of manuscripts

Manuscripts are named after their owners (for example, John Rylands or Chester Beatty), or the place where they were discovered (for example, Sinaiticus, Alexandrinus), or the place where they are housed (for example, Vaticanus). Individual manuscripts within such collections are distinguished from each other by a numbering system.

had emerged. Jewish scholars were eager to establish an agreed and universal text that would end the circulation of different versions within individual communities, in order to facilitate unity and communication between communities.

Safeguarding the text

Eventually, groups of scholars appeared who were dedicated to preserving this universal text, and, between AD 600 and 1000, these scholars (who became known as the Masoretes) began to add marks to the Hebrew consonantal text. Their aim was to record the oral traditions that surrounded the reading and teaching of the Old Testament. As they copied texts, they used a meticulous system of marks (such as dots over words) to draw attention to grammatical issues. They added marginal readings where something was considered wrong or misleading, in

preference to altering the consonantal text itself. They also kept statistics to measure the texts and words in various sections and parts in order to check that nothing had been omitted or inserted by accident in the process of copying. One of the best manuscripts from this period is the Aleppo Codex, dated c. AD 930, which clearly shows the vocalization (the vowel marks added to the original consonantal Hebrew text) provided by the Masoretes. It is remarkable that, when we compare the consonantal text that the Masoretes worked with to the text from the second century BC found at Qumran, the agreement is approximately 95 per cent.

The transmission of the New Testament

There are over 5,000 handwritten texts of the Greek New Testament dating from between the second century AD and the time when Erasmus produced the first printed edition in 1516. Their large number is evidence of the demand for copies of the New Testament text as the Christian gospel spread. The early manuscripts became the basis for other early translations of the New Testament into languages including Coptic, Syriac, Latin and Ethiopic, all of which were completed by the sixth century.

New Testament manuscripts fall into three categories:

Papyri

This is the oldest group of manuscripts, written on papyrus.

◆ The earliest papyrus manuscript is the John Rylands manuscript, containing parts of John 18, which dates to early in the second century and was published in 1935.

◆ Other important manuscripts include the Chester Beatty papyri (Gospels, Acts and Paul's letters) and the Bodmer papyri (Luke and John), both dated c. AD 200.

Uncials

These manuscripts are written on parchment and use a script that resembles our capital letters, without spaces or punctuation, which was the preferred style of writing in early literary texts. These date from the fourth century onwards and often contain the whole Bible. It is clear that the Old Testament and the New Testament were transmitted together from this point onwards, marking the church's conviction that both were to be viewed as scripture.

Codex Sinaiticus (dated in the second half of the fourth century) contains the whole Bible (plus a couple of other Christian texts: the Shepherd of Hermas and the Epistle of Barnabas).

Codex Alexandrinus (fifth century) contains the whole Bible (though some parts are now missing) plus two short letters: 1 and 2 Clement.

Codex Vaticanus (mid-fourth century) contains the whole Bible (though some parts are now missing).

Minuscules

These manuscripts are in a cursive script and, apart from a few eleventh- and twelfth-century manuscripts, date from the thirteenth to the fifteenth centuries. They are written on paper. On the whole they contain small sections of text.

Other evidence of the Greek text of the New Testament can be found in the church's lectionaries (see glossary), in the writings of the early church fathers and of course in the renditions offered by the early Bible translations. Taken together, all this evidence suggests a uniform text with only marginal variations. The care exerted with the Old Testament and its transmission was also applied to the New Testament text as it too was copied and circulated to

Above: Hebrew Bible Aleppo Codex – the earliest manuscript containing the complete text of the Hebrew Bible, dating from the 10th century AD.

Left: The Dead Sea, taken from the Judean desert cliffs.

Portrait of Jerome – the 4th-century translator of the Bible into Latin – from a French church.

meet the demands of the growing Christian communities.

Bible translation

The history of Bible translation is intertwined with the history of the geographical spread first of all of the Jewish people and then later of the Christian church. In other words, the translation of the Bible was driven by the demand for it.

Of the 6,912 languages spoken in the world, 2,426 have some or all of the Bible. Translation is now in progress into 1,953 languages, according to statistics released in December 2007 by Wycliffe Bible Translators.

- ◆ Before the start of the third century BC, most of the Old Testament was already translated into Aramaic. These translations became known as Targums and were really a loose version (paraphrase/interpretation) of the Hebrew text.

- ◆ The Septuagint (Greek translation of the Old Testament) appeared in the second to first centuries BC as Jews began to reside in Greek cities and towns.

- ◆ After that further Aramaic, Syriac (the Peshitta), Coptic (the first Christians in Egypt spoke Coptic) and Latin (Vulgate) versions began to appear. The Latin version translated by Jerome in the fourth century was dominant until the decline of the Roman empire. It remained the standard Bible in Europe until the Reformation (see glossary).

The task of translating any text into a new language is full of difficulties. Perhaps these difficulties are particularly obvious when you are dealing with a collection

of texts that are drawn together from a lengthy period of history and treated as sacred. The sorts of issues that face translators include:

- ◆ how far you should translate word for word, or try to express a meaning in the target language by a phrase that has an equivalent, though not identical, meaning to that in the source language;

- ◆ whether you should be loyal to the original meanings of words when they make no sense in the language of the translation;

- whether identical words in a text should be translated consistently;

- how word play, alliteration, poetry and puns should be represented in translation;

- how much the structure of the original language should dictate the structure of the translated text;

- how much good literary style should affect the final translation;

- how contemporary the style should be in the language you are translating into, and how far accuracy should be sacrificed to be easily understood by the readers for whom you are translating the text.

Throughout the centuries the painstaking work of translation has been undertaken by individuals and organizations in the attempt to meet people's desire to read the Bible in their own language. Present Bible translations rely on examining the most reliable manuscripts available today. Like those who first preserved the Old Testament centuries ago, contemporary translators want to preserve the Bible, circulate it and make sure that it is understood in diverse cultures, in different geographical locations, and in ever-changing times.

The canon of the Bible

The word 'canon' means 'measuring stick', 'rule' or 'standard'. It is used to describe the list of texts collected in the Bible. Christians

assert that these texts are the 'rule' of the Christian faith (see glossary, **canon**).

The canon of the Old Testament
Although the origins of the books of the Old Testament and their assembly are

Interior of a Scriptorium, 16th-century Spanish painting by the School of Segovia.

The history of the English Bible

Eighth century: Venerable Bede translated John's Gospel into Old English.

c. 890: King Alfred translated parts of Exodus, Psalms and Acts into Old English.

900/1000: The interlinear Old English translation was added to Latin Lindisfarne Gospels.

Abbot Aelfric translated the first seven books of the Old Testament into Old English.

1380s: The entire Bible in English was completed by followers of John Wycliffe (1320–1384).

1456: An edition of the Latin Vulgate Bible was the first complete book printed in the Western world, by Gutenberg in Germany.

1516: Erasmus produced a printed Greek edition of the New Testament. He accompanied it with a new Latin version.

1526: Tyndale's first printed New Testament in English appeared (based on Jerome's Latin Vulgate, Luther's German translation and Greek manuscripts).

1535: Miles Coverdale's complete English Bible was published, relying on Tyndale's work.

1537: The Thomas Matthew Bible was printed – the first English Bible printed in England (also strongly influenced by Tyndale).

1539: Thomas Cromwell commissioned Coverdale to produce the first English Bible sanctioned by the Church of England, the Great Bible, which was appointed for use in churches.

1560: The Geneva Bible was published: an English Bible in Roman type with the text divided into verses.

1611: The King James Version (KJV or Authorized Version) commissioned by King James I was produced.

1885: The Revised Version appeared, which gave attention to recently uncovered texts and manuscripts.

hidden in distant times and traditions, it is clear that the canon was divided into three parts from an early point: the Law, the Writings and the Prophets. By the time of the Qumran community all the present books of the Old Testament were carefully preserved,[2] and certainly most writers agree about the contents of the Old Testament canon by the first century AD. The only books about which there was any uncertainty were Esther, the Song of Songs and Ruth. Josephus (AD 37–100) shows us that the idea of a canon was already in place during his lifetime. In fact the Old Testament canon was possibly already a closed list by 200 BC, although some would argue that it remained open in Jesus' lifetime and was only settled at an early church council held at Jamnia in AD 90.

The Apocrypha

This word means 'hidden' or 'secret' and is used as a collective term to refer to a range of texts that emerged between 200 BC and AD 200. Over the period of Christian history there has been some dispute concerning whether or not these texts should be included in the Bible. They are similar to biblical material and were probably stored alongside Old Testament scrolls. They are preserved in Greek although they may have had earlier Hebrew or Aramaic forms. They are found in Roman Catholic versions of the Bible and were part of the Greek Old Testament of the first century. This explains why New Testament writers sometimes seem to allude to these texts (see, for example, Hebrews, Jude and

The Roman Catholic Church describes the additional Old Testament books as 'Deuterocanonical' (belonging to a second canon) and has never argued that they were part of the Jewish canon. However, the Protestant churches reacted strongly to the inclusion of these additional texts in the Old Testament and insisted that they should be excluded from the canon.

What is certain is that these additional texts do have *historical* value. They offer evidence of the continued use of literary forms present in the Old Testament and bear witness to the ongoing story of faith between the Old and the New Testaments. They also provide us with a framework for interpreting the New Testament in the light of the events that immediately post-dated the Old Testament and preceded the New Testament itself.

Flavius Josephus, the Jewish historian, is depicted in this 19th-century print by R. Lunn.

possibly Romans 1 and 2). In the fourth century an early Bible scholar, Jerome (see glossary, **Vulgate**), used the term 'apocryphal' and said these books were not to be considered authoritative parts of the Old Testament because they are not in the Jewish Bible. He added that they were still edifying if read by people who were wise and understanding.

The Roman Catholic Church and the Apocrypha

During the Reformation, the Roman Catholic Church confirmed the place of most of these books within the Old Testament, stating at the Council of Trent (1546) (see glossary) that the Old Testament contained forty-six books.

The canon of the New Testament

From the early days of the church, the first Christians started to preserve certain texts. At first they concentrated on the sayings of Jesus himself. We know that collections of these sayings explain some of the word-for-word overlap in the Gospel accounts. The 'gospel of Thomas', which contains a list of Jesus' sayings, was sometimes referred to by church leaders in the second century. The words and writings of the apostles (see glossary) also gained early recognition. In fact apostolic authorship (or indeed connection to an apostle) became an early test of authoritative standing. Gradually, the church sifted through the wealth of writings about Jesus, and the New Testament

Contents of the Apocrypha

Amounting to one quarter of the length of the Old Testament:

- 1 Esdras (or 3rd Ezra): similar material to Ezra;
- 2 Esdras (or 4th Ezra): an apocalyptic text;
- Tobit: a story of a man's piety;
- Judith: a story of a woman who uses charm to defeat the Assyrian general Holofernes;
- Additions to Esther: these bring additional religious overtones to the Old Testament story;
- Wisdom of Solomon: a first-century BC Greek ethical and rhetorical work;
- Ecclesiasticus: the wisdom song of Jesus ben Sira, c. 180 BC;
- Additions to Jeremiah: Baruch including the Letter of Jeremiah: a wisdom book plus an attack on idolatry;
- Additions to Daniel: Susanna, Bel and the Dragon, the Song of the Three Holy Children;
- Prayer of Manasseh: based on 2 Chronicles 33:13 and 19;
- 1 Maccabees: a historical account of the Maccabean revolt;
- 2 Maccabees: a moral commentary on 1 Maccabees.

Note that Roman Catholic Bibles do not contain 1 and 2 Esdras or the Prayer of Manasseh; they also omit other texts such as 3 and 4 Maccabees and Psalm 151.

canon began to take shape. By about AD 100 the list of Paul's letters was settled; by AD 150 the four Gospels were agreed. The church in Rome drew up its own list of the contents of the New Testament in AD 200 (the Muratorian Canon). This list omitted Hebrews and 3 John but included the Revelation of Peter and the Wisdom of Solomon. It also discusses a short allegorical tale called the Shepherd of Hermas. This was a popular story with many similarities to modern books like John Bunyan's *Pilgrim's Progress*. The leaders at Rome said the Shepherd was acceptable for private reading but should not be read as part of public worship. For some time there remained a little uncertainty, especially about Hebrews, the shorter epistles and Revelation. But by the beginning of the fourth century there was widespread agreement, although some hesitancy about letters such as 2 and 3 John and Jude remained.

By the time of the Council of Carthage (AD 397) the present New Testament canon had been affirmed in the West, with the same collection affirmed by Athanasius in the East in AD 367. From time to time, however, people still debate the books which were at some time in their history on the fringes of the canon.

A continuing task

This chapter has highlighted matters relating to the emergence of the Bible. The task of understanding the history of the text continues as new manuscripts come to light. The task of translating the Bible also continues. There is a wide range of English versions to choose from, but many people do not yet have the complete Bible, or even part of it, in their own language. For those of us who do, the rest of this book should be read alongside a reliable version. As we look at the Bible and its contents in more detail, it is instructive to remember the great sacrifice made by those who, throughout the centuries, have worked to make the Bible accessible.

Without their tireless endeavours – and in some cases the sacrifice of their lives – our understanding of human history in biblical times, and our understanding of the Christain faith and its development, would be so much poorer. It is because of them that it is possible to continue the journey and discover more answers to the question 'What is the Bible?'.

Far left: Caravaggio's *Judith and Holofernes*, c. 1599, based on the story from the Apocrypha.

Left: Statue of the Good Shepherd, dating from the early 3rd century AD. The shepherd is an image also used in other biblical texts. For example, in John 10 Jesus describes himself as the Good Shepherd.

The writing of the Bible

| 11th century BC ← | Old Testament → | 2nd century BC |
| AD 47 ← | New Testament → | AD 100 |

The stories of the Bible

| 2000 BC ← | Old Testament → | 4th century BC |
| 6 BC ← | New Testament → | AD 100 |

CHAPTER

The World of the Bible

The diverse origins of biblical documents

It is necessary to examine the background of a piece of literature closely if it is to be understood fully. The origins of a document are important to discovering its meaning and significance. With the Bible, it is important to recognize that it contains literature that has come together over a long period of time. We must also remember that its various sections are set in different places, each with their own distinctive cultural features.

This chapter attempts to respect these diverse origins while at the same time providing a contextual framework that facilitates

Cultural and religious diversity provide the background to the biblical texts. On the right, a 3rd-century BC Sumerian statuette thought to represent the god Abu, from the Abu Temple at the Mesopotamian site of Tell Asmar.

an appropriate understanding and interpretation of the whole biblical text. This will be undertaken by examining the historical, geographical and cultural settings of the Bible.

Historical setting[1]

There are two ways of thinking about the Bible's historical setting.

◆ First, we can think about the historical setting in which the Bible books were written. In other words, the focus is upon *the authors of the biblical books* in an attempt to try to understand what circumstances the authors faced and how those circumstances influenced their writings.

Most scholars now agree that the contents of the Old Testament were written down and collected into their present form between the eleventh century BC and the second century BC. So their authors and collectors span a 1,000-year period. In contrast, the writing of the New Testament spans no more than a sixty-year period.

Within these periods of time political, economic, religious and cultural changes occurred.

◆ Second, the historical background can also be investigated in terms of the time-span of the accounts contained within the Bible. Here the focus is upon *the stories and events of the biblical books*. This approach, of course, extends the period of interest even further. Even if the first eleven chapters of Genesis are excluded, it adds another 1,000-year period (from the patriarchs [see glossary] onwards) to the scope of the Old Testament and at least another fifty years to the New Testament (covering the period from Jesus' birth onwards).

With these timescales in mind, the attempt to consider the Bible's setting is complicated further by even more political, economic, religious and cultural changes.

The details of the biblical stories are covered here in the chapters on the Old Testament and the New Testament (see chapters 4 and 5).

For the sake of convenience, in the table that follows the Bible accounts are divided into blocks of time, and some of the main features of the history of these times are highlighted. What is clear is that the biblical story is set in a world characterized by unrest, uncertainty and unpredictable change, dominated by the competing interests of world powers (although in the first century Roman peace brought a period of security). These powers, and other lesser nations (see chapter 7) with whom they came into contact, shaped each other's history in a time of cultural advance and development. This was a period of rapid change, and the world we encounter at the end of biblical times, the New Testament world, would be unrecognizable from the perspective of the pre-historic times described in the Bible's earliest accounts. The focus of the Old Testament story is one nation's history within the tumult of the ancient world, but that nation's history nevertheless provides the religious and cultural backdrop for the New Testament period.

Biblical books and time-spans

Reading the Bible can sometimes be challenging because different biblical books cover different time-spans. Although usually the longer the book is, the greater the period of time it covers, this is not always the case. Here are some examples of the lengths of time covered by the books of the Bible:

Genesis 12–50	300 years
Numbers	38 years
Deuteronomy	1 month
Joshua	15 years
Judges	335 years
Jonah	1 month
2 Chronicles	384 years
Ezra/Nehemiah	138 years
Esther	9 years
Matthew and Luke	36 years
Mark and John	3 years

Note that the Psalms also reflect a long period of history from approximately 1000 BC until 250 BC; the final collection of these songs was probably compiled c. 250 BC.

Dates	Biblical events	Historical developments
To 2000 BC	Prehistory ◆ creation ◆ first human life ◆ Job (possibly the earliest book to be written down; set in the world in which the patriarchs emerged)	**Stone Age to Early Bronze Age** Ancient civilizations emerge: the beginnings of the historical period of the Ancient Near East. ◆ Sumerian people live in Mesopotamia (3000 BC onwards); it is not united like Egypt but consists of rival city-states; written records are scarce before 2500 BC. ◆ Egyptian culture emerges (3000 BC); during the Pyramid Age (2600 BC) Egyptian culture is shaped around the divine-human king or pharaoh. ◆ The Babylonians appear (c. 3000 BC); the Babylonian dialect of the Akkadian language eventually becomes the language of international exchange. ◆ Less evidence exists, but cultures also emerge in Elam/Iran, in Asia Minor, and in Syria and Palestine. (A written script develops in Ebla around 2400 BC.)
2000 BC onwards	Abraham and the other patriarchs	**Middle Bronze Age** ◆ Babylonian empire becomes increasingly powerful (1850 BC). ◆ By 1800 BC Assyria is one of the most powerful nations in the region. ◆ Hurrians, Amorites and other nomadic peoples start to settle in Canaan. ◆ Hittite empire (1650–1200 BC). (Hittites contribute a great deal to our knowledge of this period as they had a strong sense of historiography.)
1500 BC onwards	◆ Moses (born c. 1350–1300 BC) ◆ Israelites leave Egypt ◆ entry into Canaan ◆ Judges	**Late Bronze to Early Iron Age** ◆ Tutankhamun dies c.1350 BC. ◆ Assyrian empire – twelfth to seventh centuries BC. ◆ Philistines (one of the 'sea peoples') emerge in the eastern Mediterranean region (1200 BC).

Dates	Biblical events	Historical developments
1000 BC onwards	Israel is under monarchy. ◆ Saul, David, Solomon ◆ kingdom of Israel divides (931 BC) (see chapter 4, **The Israelites divide**) ◆ both kingdoms fall (722 and 587 BC) ◆ exile	**Late Iron Age to Persian Age** ◆ Rise of Damascus/Aram (950 BC). ◆ Assyrian domination spreads from Mesopotamia to Palestine (750 BC). ◆ Re-emergence of Egypt (the Egyptians drive out the Assyrians in 650 BC). ◆ Re-emergence of Babylon (605 BC); but Babylon then falls to Cyrus in 539 BC. ◆ Persian empire (550–330 BC); led by the Achaemenids, who treat their subjects with tolerance and respect. Cyrus (560–530 BC) allows the rebuilding of the Temple in Jerusalem. Cyrus is followed by Cambyses (530–522 BC) and Darius I (522–486 BC).
500 BC onwards	Return to Jerusalem	Period of prosperity for the Persian empire under Darius. Aramaic becomes the official language of the empire, and communications are improved as trade routes and road links develop.
400 BC onwards	Intertestamental period	◆ Persian period continues; the empire is unrivalled, but it begins to disintegrate and is finally overcome by Alexander the Great in 333 BC. *The end of the historical period of the Ancient Near East as Greek culture takes over.* **Hellenistic Age** Hellenistic period (333–166 BC) ◆ Alexander the Great (356–323 BC) defeats the Persian armies in 333 BC. ◆ Greek Ptolemaic rulers control Egypt, and Seleucid rulers control Syria and Mesopotamia (323–198 BC). ◆ Seleucid rulers take control of Palestine (198 BC). ◆ Reign of Antiochus IV Epiphanes (175–164 BC). ◆ Antiochus desecrates the Jerusalem Temple (167 BC). ◆ Maccabean revolt (167–164 BC); leadership of Judas Maccabeus (166–160 BC).

Dates	Biblical events	Historical developments
400 BC onwards	Intertestamental period	**Hasmonean Period** Hasmonean period (164–63 BC) **Roman Age** ♦ Roman period (63 BC): Pompey captures Jerusalem in 63 BC, killing priests and desecrating the Temple. ♦ Julius Caesar is murdered in 44 BC. ♦ Egypt is taken by the Romans (on the deaths of Mark Antony and Cleopatra in 30 BC).
5 BC – AD 3 onwards	Jesus' lifetime ♦ Born c. 5 BC ♦ Public ministry AD 25–30 ♦ Died AD 30–33	♦ Greek civilization develops under Roman rule. ♦ Jewish Diaspora accelerates; there are especially large communities in Alexandria and Rome. ♦ Jewish community around the Dead Sea at Qumran. ♦ Herod the Great becomes ruler of Palestine (37–34 BC). ♦ Pontius Pilate (AD 26–36) is Roman prefect of Judea.
to 100 AD	♦ the church is established. ♦ Paul's ministry.	♦ Emperor Nero (AD 54–68): fire destroys Rome in AD 64. ♦ Temple in Jerusalem is destroyed AD 70. ♦ Emperors Vespasian and Titus build the Colosseum in Rome (AD 69–81). ♦ Emperor Domitian (AD 81–96).

Geographical setting

As well as being a historical period (2000 BC to 330 BC), the term 'Ancient Near East' is used to refer to the area from Asia Minor (Turkey) in the north to the Persian Gulf and Egypt in the south; with modern Iran in the east and the Mediterranean Sea in the west. This area has varied physical features:

♦ major rivers (Nile, Euphrates, Tigris, Jordan);

♦ corresponding large valleys;

♦ mountainous regions;

♦ coastal plains;

♦ desert regions.

These physical features played an important role in the region's political and cultural development. For example:

- Trade routes became an important factor in attracting the interest of diverse people groups to this region.

- Natural boundaries (such as rivers, valleys, mountains and hills) played their part in warfare and political developments.

- Varied terrain and natural irrigation meant that diverse agricultural activities developed.

The land of Palestine

Palestine lies between Egypt (to the south) and Mesopotamia (to the north) and has the Mediterranean Sea to the west. It is cut in two by the River Jordan, which runs its length. Its location between the two great civilizations in the Fertile Crescent (the valley region served by the Nile, Tigris and Euphrates) meant that Palestine assumed centre stage in biblical times. It is approximately 600 kilometres (373 miles) long and, at its widest point, 120 kilometres (75 miles) wide. Its physical features, running from west to east, are:

- The coastal plain: containing Mount Carmel, the Plain of Sharon and, in the south, the Sinai desert with its central mountainous region reaching over 700 metres).

- The central mountains (or 'western mountains'): in the north the mountains reach 1,500 metres, rising to over 2,000

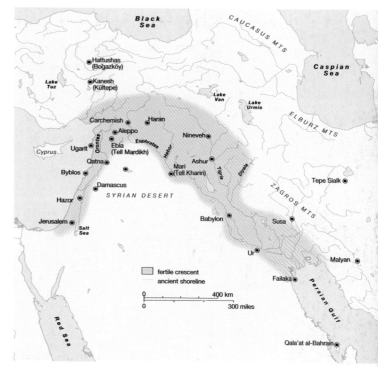

metres in the Lebanon range. Continuing further south the lower mountains of Galilee are to be found (including Mount Tabor). South of the Galilean range is the valley of Jezreel (which provides a break in the mountainous regions) and then the mountains of Samaria (the highest peak being Jebel Asur at just over 1,000 metres). The central mountainous area continues southwards to form the plateau of Benjamin, followed by the hills of Judah, including Hebron (1,000 metres). South of Beersheba are the gentle hills

Above: Map of the Ancient Near East, c. 2000 BC.

Left: The Colosseum in Rome, Italy. It was the largest ampitheatre in the Roman empire and was built AD 70–82.

27

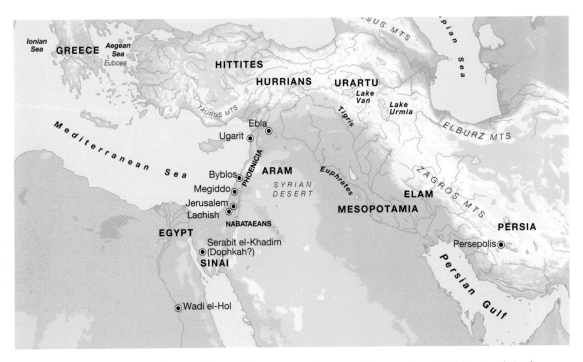

Map of the Middle East showing the location of Palestine between Mesopotamia and Egypt.

Top right: Egyptian wall painting of Rameses II, dressed for war.

Map, right : Ancient Egypt, with key cities shown.

Far Right: The Sphinx and Chefren Pyramid, Giza, Egypt.

of the Negev, followed by the mountains of Sinai which, unlike the other central mountains, increase in height as they spread southwards.

◆ The valley region (the 'Rift Valley'): from north to south – the valley of the River Orontes is followed by the valley area between the Lebanon ranges, then the Jordan Valley between the Sea of Galilee and the Dead Sea. The Jordan Valley and the Dead Sea are below sea level.

◆ The inland mountains (or 'eastern mountains'): from north to south – the Anti-Lebanon range, including Mount

Hermon (over 2,800 metres), in the south; the Bashan, Gilead and Moabite ridges (all with peaks over 1,000 metres); the mountains of Edom (with two peaks reaching over 1,700 metres). To the east of the mountains lie desert areas.

The diverse physical make-up of Palestine means that temperatures differ from place to place. The summer is hot; the winter is cooler and wetter, but sunny days still dominate. Snow only lasts in the higher mountain ranges such as Lebanon and Mount Hermon.

Egypt

Egypt is dominated by the River Nile, which is about 6,600 kilometres (4,100 miles) in length from its origin, Lake Victoria in east Africa, to its delta at the Mediterranean Sea. It winds down through the dry region of modern Sudan and the eastern Sahara Desert before reaching the contrasting swampy delta region. The Nile provides irrigation and agricultural possibilities in the desert and was consequently the main reason for Egypt's strength, stability and relative well-being in biblical times. Egypt's four main regions are:

♦ the delta region: a wide expanse of marshland stretching from Cairo to the sea;

♦ the Nile Valley (formerly Upper Egypt): the narrow river valley between Cairo and Aswan;

◆ the western desert (or the 'Libyan Desert', part of the Sahara): with a few oases, making up nearly three-quarters of Egypt's territory;

◆ the eastern desert (or 'Arabian Desert'): with the Red Sea at its heart and characterized by mountains and wadis.

Egypt has a typical desert climate, with the raised eastern side of the Nile generally a little cooler than the west. A few trees grow, along with plentiful supplies of papyrus plants, in the Nile delta but otherwise the region is mainly barren.

Mesopotamia

In biblical times this name was given to the land lying between the rivers Euphrates and Tigris. Both these rivers have their sources in the mountains of eastern Asia Minor (which include the volcanic peak of Mount Ararat, over 5,000 metres). The climate of Mesopotamia is very similar to that of Palestine, and the southern region has more vegetation than the northern territory. It is, again, only the rivers that enable land in the region to be fertile.

Persia

Persia consists of a large plateau surrounded by mountains which reach a height of over 5,600 metres in the Elburz range that runs south from the Caspian Sea. The plateau contains two desert areas which are barren because the surrounding mountains block the rain: the Great Desert in the north and the Desert of Lot in the south.

The Persian territories have a diversity of temperature and vegetation. Elam and Media became important cultural centres because of their favourable climate and easy access to other territories.

Asia Minor

This area, from which the Hittites originated, links Asia and Europe. It is another plateau surrounded by mountains and is located between the northern coast of the Mediterranean Sea and the southern coast of the Black Sea. Its most important region is that of Mysia and Lydia. In the coastal region by the Black Sea the climate is cool, but the southern coast has a Mediterranean climate. The surrounding mountains mean that the weather in the middle is more challenging and vegetation is sparser. Asia Minor's history has been greatly affected by its physical geography: its struggle towards unity was hampered by the inaccessibility of some areas because of the mountains. In New Testament times the city of Ephesus became prominent, and attracted the missionary activities of the apostle Paul (see chapter 6, **Paul**). The island of Patmos (see chapter 8, **Patmos**), where the apostle John (see chapter 6, **John**) was exiled, is located off the south-west coast of Asia Minor.

Greece

Sea and mountains dominate Greece and its islands. Four-fifths of Greece consists of mountainous areas, with a few peaks reaching over 2,000 metres. The sea produces a mild climate, although on some of the highest mountains temperatures can drop below freezing. Greece has few rivers but abundant vegetation. The apostle Paul visited Athens, the centre of Greek culture.

Italy

Italy is also dominated by sea and by mountains, which include the Alps in the north, continuing into the Apennine range that runs down the length of the country as far as Sicily. The mountain areas have varied climates but to the south of the Alps the climate is mainly Mediterranean.

Other regions visited by Jesus

Decapolis

An area east of the Jordan, outside Palestine (see Matthew 8:28–34; Mark 5:1–20; Mark 7:31; Luke 8:26–39), this region was made up of ten cities (including Philadelphia, Damascus and Gadara), occupying land on the major trade routes to the Mediterranean Sea. The cities were dominated by Greek culture and benefited from a degree of interdependence. In Paul's day Christian people were already to be found in this region.

Tyre and Sidon

Jesus visited these cities in the province of Syria, to the north of Palestine (see Matthew 15:21; Mark 7:31). Both cities were situated on the coast and became important because of their location on major trade routes (including the way to Damascus).

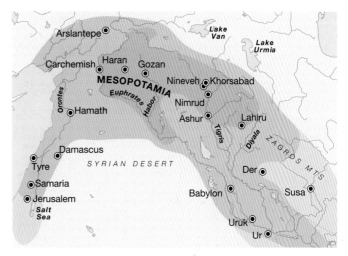

Map above: Ancient Mesopotamia.

Cultural setting

Cultural development and change during the biblical era was wide-ranging. The history of Israel exemplifies the way in which divergent circumstances dictated the cultural development both of Israel itself and of the surrounding nations. For example, the people moved from a nomadic lifestyle to settled farming communities and from tribal organization to monarchy, followed by occupation and oppression. But throughout these changing circumstances it is possible to identify some common cultural elements that characterized the region.

Writing

Corresponding to the large number of population groups in the Ancient Near East, languages and scripts were also profuse. The earliest scripts were

cuneiform from Mesopotamia and hieroglyphics from Egypt. Much more is known about early Egyptian culture than about Mesopotamian culture, though, because the documents preserved in Egypt are prolific and often have a historical orientation.

Early writing materials included stone tablets, clay, potsherds and animal skins. In Egypt the art of writing developed quickly with the development of papyrus but in other places written documentation was much slower to emerge. Early examples of writing exist from Ebla and Byblos but apart from these it was not until the second millennium BC that writing appeared in Syria-Palestine. The first true alphabet system (based on consonantal sounds) was produced by the Canaanites at around this time and was then passed on by the Phoenicians. The Israelites, Arameans and others started producing written records in the first millennium BC. Some time after the eighth century BC the Greeks added vowel signs, and writing was reversed to read from left to right in the West. The texts of the Old Testament used Hebrew and Aramaic, whereas the New Testament is written in Greek, though still incorporating Aramaic elements (see chapter 1, **Biblical Aramaic**).

Letter writing

Letter writing is mentioned in many Old Testament passages (see, for example, 2 Samuel 11:14; 1 Kings 21:8; 2 Kings 5:5–7; 10:1). Letters were written on clay tablets, animal skins, palm leaves or papyrus. In Persia, letters were often rolled into scrolls, covered and sealed (see Daniel 12:4, 9). Written edicts were circulated as systems for official communication developed (see Esther 3:12–15; 8:9–14). Evidence from the fifth century BC in Egypt suggests that wooden tablets covered with wax were used for writing: a stylus would scratch characters into the wax. Much of the New Testament is actually written in the form of letters which conform to the normal conventions of the time (see chapter 3, **Letters**). Most of the New Testament letters, however, are much longer than average letters of their day, which tended to be around the length of 2 and 3 John. From Ezra's time onwards, professional scribes were responsible for copying the Law, as well as reading it, interpreting it and teaching it.

Justice in Old Testament times

Ancient communities showed a keen appreciation of the need for justice and laws as a means to safeguard community life. The Ten Commandments show similarities with other ancient law codes – and, of course, the ninth commandment, 'You shall not bear false witness', was intended as a prohibition against perjury. The basic principle of law in Old Testament times was that the punishment should fit the crime. In other words, justice means restricting punishment to a level commensurate with the crime; excessive revenge was not pursued. Officials of justice included elders, judges, magistrates, Levites and various governors: Moses (Exodus 18:13–

27) acted as a judge. Their job was to ensure that everyone was treated fairly and that the courts showed no partiality. Two witnesses were required in court for a guilty verdict to be possible.

Left: An example of Egyptian hieroglyphs.

Above: Torah scrolls.

Justice in New Testament times

In the New Testament period, courts were ordered places with their own etiquette. So, for example, judges sat down while the accused stood before them (see Matthew 27:11; Acts 26:6). Paul advises Christians that they should be able to settle disputes without going to court (1 Corinthians 6:1–7), although he shows respect for the justice system. In exercising his rights as a Roman citizen he appeals to Caesar to intervene in the processes of local justice (Acts 25:11–12; 26:31–32).

Slavery

Foreign slaves were used in building

Forms of punishment in biblical times

Capital punishment: burning alive, crucifixion, beheading, cutting into pieces, drowning, hanging, sawing in half, being thrown from a rock, stoning.

Other forms of punishment: binding and fettering, forced labour, hanging by the hand, destruction of the home or other property, mutilation, ostracism, imprisonment, paying fines or compensation, plucking of the hair, scourging.

projects and for hard labour in Ancient Near Eastern communities. In Palestine and Syria slaves were more like house servants and they were generally treated well, as family members. The early books of the Bible that regulate Jewish community life establish very clear instructions about the treatment of slaves. Slaves were treated as people in their own right; they could expect days off and had some hope of being freed. Jewish laws about slaves were based on Israel's own experience of slavery in Egypt (see Exodus 21; 23:12; Deuteronomy 5:12–15; 15:15; 23:15–16).

In New Testament times slaves were an integral part of the way Roman society worked. Some slaves were educated, holding responsible positions managing businesses and the like. The New Testament letter to Philemon is a plea to him to treat a young slave called Onesimus kindly even though he has run away.

Money

In the earliest biblical times payment was made in goods rather than money, but as early as the stories of Abraham and Joseph the use of pieces of silver was known; copper and gold were also used to pay for land, goods and services.

The first standardized coinage system came from Asia Minor (c. 700 BC). In the Persian period other coins appeared, including the daric, the drachma, the mina and the shekel. In New Testament times the denarius, talent, drachma, pound, assarion and penny are mentioned. Roman emperors started to place images on coinage: sometimes natural pictures (an olive branch, palm trees, barley) but increasingly the image of the emperor himself.

Warfare and weaponry

From the earliest Old Testament passages there are mentions of weapons being in use, although they are rarely described. Most of our evidence comes from archaeological discoveries. One important source of information about New Testament times is Ephesians 6:10–17, which speaks figuratively of the armour Christians have for the spiritual warfare in which they are engaged. Paul mentions here a belt, a breastplate, shoes, a shield and a helmet. Other pieces of military equipment mentioned in the Bible include axes, arrows, javelins, nets, quivers, sling-shots and spears.

Marriage

Early in the Old Testament it was common for men to have more than one wife, but by Ezra's time the assumption in Israelite society was monogamy. Girls and young men were married young (probably 12 or 13 being the minimum age), and parents took the responsibility for finding their offspring partners. A period of betrothal preceded marriage: this was a binding agreement with legal status. Men had to pay for their bride by working for her family or by giving them a monetary amount. Weddings incorporated a banquet, and the couple wore elaborate clothes. The festivities seem regularly to have lasted for at least a week. The brother-in-law of a childless widow was required to marry her and, to ensure the brother's line of descent, their firstborn son would be considered the child of the dead brother. Children were understood as a blessing, a gift from God. The firstborn son assumed the father's authority over the family and would receive a double portion of the father's inheritance. Names given to children (and, later, name changes) were significant, often reflecting the experiences or feelings of a parent, or the child's characteristics or the role that he or she would fulfil.

Death and burial

The final words a person spoke before death were often given great significance. To die in old age was considered a blessing from God. In Egypt, bodies were embalmed. Jewish burial rites involved washing the body and applying perfumed ointment before wrapping the body in cloths. Burial was the norm rather than burning (which was reserved for criminals); natural caves or man-made carved tombs were used as graves. Poorer people simply covered bodies with earth. Burial usually took place on the day of death because of the warm climate. Death was marked by rituals involving professional mourners. Outward signs of mourning included tearing clothes, wearing sackcloth, shaving the head, fasting, and playing flutes and singing laments.

Housing

In the earliest times people sheltered in caves. The patriarchs lived in tents, and these continued to be used for some time after the Israelites had entered Canaan, especially by herdsmen tending cattle or those engaged in warfare. The tents were probably made of goatskins. City dwellings had already developed at this time, for example at Jericho, Sodom and Hazor, but the nomadic lifestyle of the patriarchs meant that temporary dwellings were more appropriate. Early houses in Palestine were made of mud bricks and wood. Most houses had flat roofs, accessed by an outside staircase, and lattice windows. Poor people shared their houses with livestock, all together in a single room. Furniture was sparse, although there were considerable differences between the

Forms of transport in biblical times

Walking; animals: camels, donkeys, horses, mules; vehicles: wagons, caravans, carts, chariots; sea travel: warships, merchant ships, passenger ships.

Top Left: Ancient Roman denarii coins.

Far Left: A fourth dynasty funerary vase of Hetepheres.

Right: The Code of Hammurabi, c.1750 BC, was discovered at Susa, Iran. This stone pillar depicts the god Shamash dictating his laws to Hammurabi, King of Babylon.

Below: The Rosetta Stone, now housed in the British Museum. It shows text in Greek and in Egyptian hieroglyphics. This enabled J. F. Champollion and Thomas Young to decipher the riddle of hieroglyphics.

homes of the poor and those of the rich. Royal palaces were lavish with gold and ivory fixtures.

Clothing

The early chapters of Genesis suggest that Adam and Eve sewed fig-leaves as coverings, but this may be a metaphorical detail rather than reflecting any ancient practice. In the early period covered by the Bible simple tunics were commonplace, along with an outer cloak and sometimes an under-tunic loincloth. Belts made of cloth strips enabled the wearer to tuck the tunic in when necessary. Women's clothes were very similar to men's, although possibly of different length or colour. Women wore veils at their wedding celebrations. Early clothes were made from camel, sheep or goat hair but fine clothes were made of linen. Wealthy Egyptians wore decorated fine linen wraps with ornate headdresses and plenty of jewellery.

Archaeology: its contribution to understanding the biblical world

Archaeological discoveries, particularly over the last 200 years, have helped us to understand more about the world of the Bible. Archaeologists work on the sites of ancient towns, cities and settlements to uncover the history of the place and of the people who lived there. These sites are often raised areas ('tells' or 'mounds') which represent successive layers of history where one habitation has been built on top of another. Although archaeology will never provide all the answers to our questions, some noteworthy discoveries have been particularly helpful, enabling us to set the Bible events in their historical context.

The Rosetta Stone

The Rosetta Stone was discovered when Napoleon's armies invaded Egypt in 1798. It displays the same text in Greek and in Egyptian hieroglyphics, which enabled archaeologists to crack the code of hieroglyphics. This in turn helped us to understand a lot more about the Ancient Near Eastern world.

Gilgamesh epic

The Gilgamesh epic is an Akkadian story from the early second millennium BC which explains how Gilgamesh, a ruler in Uruk, survived a great deluge by going into an ark. There are many parallels to Genesis 6–9, although it is written from a polytheistic point of view.

Hammurabi's code

Discovered on a 2.5-metre black stone pillar this eighteenth-century BC Akkadian law code contains many parallels with Mosaic laws. It has a prologue and an epilogue and contains nearly 300 laws designed to protect the interests of the people. There are laws against theft, about hiring goods and services, and regulating marriage and family relationships.

Tutankhamun's treasures

Discovered by Howard Carter in 1922, these treasures from the burial chamber of a mid-fourteenth-century BC Egyptian pharaoh have provided us with a great deal of information about the culture of Egypt at this time.

Tell al-Amarna letters

The Tell al-Amarna letters were found in 1887. They consist of a series of clay tablets inscribed in the Akkadian cuneiform script. They date from the fourteenth century BC and were written by rulers in Canaan describing the tensions as new population groups arrived in Canaan.

Lachish letters

The Lachish letters are Hebrew documents from the early sixth century BC. They are inscribed on pottery and tell of the days in Jerusalem immediately after it was besieged by the Babylonians (588–586 BC). Lachish was a fortress city on the Palestine–Egyptian border.

Dead Sea scrolls

A shepherd discovered the Dead Sea scrolls, preserved in pottery jars, in 1947. Some scrolls are fragmentary but others are well preserved, such as the Isaiah scroll. They provide good evidence about the community rules and the leaders that governed the life of a Jewish Essene community (see chapter 7, **Essenes**).

Further reading suggestions

Paul Lawrence, *The Lion Atlas of Bible History*, Oxford: Lion, 2006.

A. R. Millard, *A Treasury of Bible Pictures*, Oxford: Lion, 1987.

M. J. Mulder and others (eds), *The World of the Bible*, Grand Rapids: Eerdmans, 1986.

What is in the Bible?

Different kinds of literature in the Bible library

The Bible contains a collection of works of literature usually called 'books'. But this label is a little misleading because some of the 'books' are in fact letters, collections of poems and songs, or collections of spoken material. It is not always easy to navigate the Bible. Not every type of writing in it can be treated in the same way. For example, poems can be read individually – they can stand alone – whereas one section of a story doesn't really make sense without the other sections. This chapter will act as a guide to the 'Bible library' and will help in the location and understanding of the various types of literature it contains.

The stories in the Bible are among the most well-known pieces of biblical literature, with fascinating twists and turns and engaging characters.

Bible stories form the basis of many popular musical works, for example Haydn's 'The Creation, An Oratorio', based on Genesis 1.

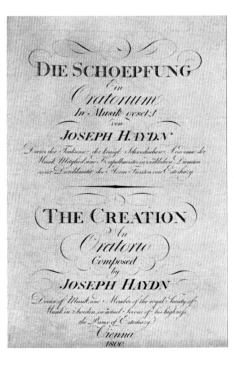

Stories

Most people love a good story that captures the imagination, draws readers into the fine details and compels them to find out what happens at the end. Most importantly, individual Bible stories are part of a bigger story: the story of God relating to and revealing himself to the created world. This overriding story, and the smaller stories it contains, is engaging because it evokes many different emotions, often stimulating empathy for characters whose

The Triumph of Mordecai, English school, c. 1870. This incident appears in Esther 6.

life experiences are comparable to our own. Bible stories can be used pedagogically because they are engaging – this perhaps explains why they make up nearly 60 per cent of the Bible and are generally speaking its most well-known parts. After all, stories are easy to pass on. They are a universal medium and appeal to young and old, male and female, rich and poor, across a diversity of cultures. Every culture has its own favourite stories and its own preferred styles of story writing.

'Story' does not imply fiction

The label 'story' does not imply fiction. In fact, most of the stories in the Bible read like true accounts of events in history. In the light of this, these parts of the Bible are sometimes referred to as 'histories' or 'narratives'. But 'story' seems an appropriate term because it serves as a reminder that the writers intend to draw in their readers. Their purpose is to involve the reader and provoke a response, not simply to give historical information. The authors of the Bible stories present their material in their own preferred style and from their own point of view. They add statements that evaluate what is going on, just as any good storyteller does. It is important to bear this in mind where one biblical account of an event differs from another. Rather than raising questions about the text's veracity, it may be better to try to understand the reasons why one author's writing differs from another's.

Understanding a Bible story

To understand a Bible story, it is useful to think particularly about four features:

◆ its setting and background;

◆ its shape (for example, its beginning, middle and end);

◆ its special features (how are characters presented? How is tension introduced?);

◆ its author's point of view.

Characters in Bible stories

Because characters are so important in stories, it is worth giving them careful attention. Sometimes characters reveal where the author's sympathies lie. This is often achieved by setting up contrasts between characters. The best biblical example of this is perhaps the contrast between Mordecai (the righteous Jew) and Haman (the evil villain) in the story of Esther; but we also have Cain and Abel, Abraham and Lot, Jacob and Esau, David and Saul, to name only a few others (see chapter 6, **Individuals in the Bible**). Some characters develop as the story unfolds and readers become interested in them, whereas others are not very intriguing because we are only told one thing about them. All these aspects of character presentation indicate the author's concerns. It is often those stories whose main character has both weaknesses and strengths (King David, for example) that are best remembered. They are more realistic and true to human experience.

are not simply biographies of Jesus but are written to persuade, and to announce to their readers that Jesus is someone worth believing in (John 20:31).

Bible stories, then, are more testimonies than biographies or straight historical records. They are included in the Bible as evidence in favour of accepting the faith to which their authors adhere.

Law

Some people wish that the entire Bible was made up of stories. Certainly the legal portions of the Old Testament have received a bad press. To modern-day ears, law is bad news because it is connected with ideas of punishment, restriction and imposed authority. Sometimes the Jewish and Christian faiths are condemned as legalistic. They have been caricatured as faiths of obedience defined only by a list of 'dos and don'ts'. Closer examination of biblical religion will reveal the nature of the authors' passion for the Law and help to reassess this caricature.

It is true that many laws are listed in the Old Testament (613 in fact) but it is worth noting that these laws occur in the story-books. In other words, laws find their place within an account of the people's journey and discovery of God. This is emphasized in Jewish Bibles, where the first five books together (the Pentateuch) are called 'the Law', or the *Torah*, to use the Hebrew word. Part of the difficulty is that there is no easy translation of this Hebrew word. 'Law' fails to convey all of its meaning. *Torah*

Reading stories

It is always better to read Bible stories in their entirety rather than break them down into smaller units. For example, it is preferable to read the stories of Joseph (Genesis 37–50), Ruth (chapters 1–4), Jesus (any one of the four Gospels) or the early church (the book of Acts) in one sitting. Stories are meant to be enjoyed – so relax and enjoy them.

Celebrations of faith

In the end, Bible stories are celebrations of faith. They announce, loudly and clearly, that in the authors' opinion God is active in the lives of individual people and in the world as a whole. The Gospel stories about Jesus seem to show this most clearly. They

Stories' location: Major collections of stories are found in Genesis, Exodus, Leviticus, Numbers, Deuteronomy, Joshua, Judges, Ruth, 1 and 2 Samuel, 1 and 2 Chronicles, Esther, Jonah, the four New Testament Gospels and Acts. Shorter passages of stories are scattered elsewhere in the Bible (for example in Isaiah and Ezra–Nehemiah).

Law location: Parts of Exodus, Leviticus, Numbers and Deuteronomy consist of law.

The story of Joseph (Genesis 37–50) is retold in Andrew Lloyd Webber's *Joseph and the Amazing Technicolor Dreamcoat*.

means 'teaching' and 'guidance', and that is what the law sections of the Bible provide. They offer guidance to a people who want to ensure that the God they trust in will bless them and be with them. So, rather than being life-restricting, the law of the *Torah* gives people security and identity. That is why the psalmist says, 'How I love your law' (Psalm 119:97).

There are four main collections of law in the Old Testament:

♦ the Book of the Covenant, including the Ten Commandments (Exodus 20–23);

♦ tabernacle laws (Exodus 25–40);

♦ laws of Leviticus (Leviticus 1–27, containing the Holiness Code in chapters 17–26);

♦ laws of Deuteronomy (Deuteronomy 12–26).

These law collections display parallels with other law codes from the Old Testament era, but also have distinctive aspects (see **Archaeology** section at the end of chapter 2, e.g., Ebla tablets; Nuzi tablets; Hammurabi code).

Within these four collections there are two types of law:

(i) Laws that are timeless standards of behaviour, often beginning 'You shall' or 'You shall not'.

The most famous example of this kind of law is the Ten Commandments in Exodus 20. It is all too easy to overlook the introduction to these commands, which makes it very clear that God gives

Covenant

The Old Testament law was given as part of a wider 'covenant' that God set up in order to initiate God's relationship with Israel. The word 'covenant' is used to describe a contractual arrangement between two parties, outlining both the responsibilities and privileges of their relationship. But when the word is applied to Israel's relationship with God it means much more than this, because, while there is mutuality, what matters is that God will be permanently committed to God's people, whatever happens. So God's covenant with Israel is of a different quality from other contractual covenants in Old Testament times:

• It will last for ever, not just for a specified period of time.
• It guarantees an eternal relationship, not just material benefits.
• It is a gift from God, not just a negotiated basis for operating.
• Its success is guaranteed by God's faithfulness, demanding an attitude of loyalty, not just appropriate behaviour.

In other words, God's covenant is not simply an agreement: it describes a state of being. Underlying the language of 'covenant' in the Bible is the principle of love; for God's covenant with God's people is a gift of love intended to provoke love in response. It is with the covenant in place that God declares, 'I am the Lord your God' (Exodus 20:2), and gives the Ten Commandments. They are therefore less commandments and more descriptions – of the proper loving response to a God who has singled out a people for relationship with himself.

them not in order to outline how people can earn favour, but because God has already called the people out of slavery and into freedom. A loving God offers people the way to enjoy life to the full by following guidance. This fact has been realized over the centuries by those countries that have based their own law codes and ethical standards on the laws of Exodus 20.

Illustration, c. 1835, depicting Moses with the tablets of the Ten Commandments, and Aaron overlooking the corrupt Jews.

Text of Leviticus 27:2–8

Speak to the Israelites and say to them: 'If anyone makes a special vow to dedicate persons to the Lord by giving equivalent values, set the value of a male between the ages of twenty and sixty at fifty shekels of silver, according to the sanctuary shekel; and if it is a female, set her value at thirty shekels. If it is a person between the ages of five and twenty, set the value of a male at twenty shekels and of a female at ten shekels. If it is a person between one month and five years, set the value of a male at five shekels of silver and that of a female at three shekels of silver. If it is a person sixty years old or more, set the value of a male at fifteen shekels and of a female at ten shekels. If anyone making the vow is too poor to pay the specified amount, he is to present the person to the priest, who will set the value for him according to what the man making the vow can afford.'

(ii) Laws which give instruction for various situations, often with the structure 'If this happens, then do this'.

This second group of laws is firmly rooted in the context of ancient Israel's religious and civil life. Such laws therefore sometimes seem quite irrelevant to today's world. There are many examples of this type of law in the regulations about purity in Leviticus and Numbers 5:1 – 10:10.

So it is best to understand the law passages in the Bible not as restrictive rules but as a way of protecting the relationship between God and God's people. It is this idea which best makes sense of the apparent criticisms of reliance on 'the law and the prophets' by Jesus himself and in Paul's writings. The law was never meant to be an end in itself. Instead it is a vehicle for God's presence, purpose and power in the world. It is in this way that Christians believe Jesus becomes the fulfilment of the law (Matthew 5:17).

Prophecy

Over the centuries there have been many famous orators. Politicians, human-rights campaigners and religious leaders such as Sir Winston Churchill, Nelson Mandela, Martin Luther King, C. H. Spurgeon and Billy Graham come to mind. If Jews in Jesus' time were asked to name a great orator, they would undoubtedly have suggested one of the Old Testament prophets. But what makes a great orator? Certainly having a powerful message and a powerful way of delivering that message are key qualities. The power of the prophets' message comes from its origin: the prophets believed that their role was to bring a message given to them by God, not one they had devised for themselves. They were God's messengers, and they employed poetry, rhetorical skill, passion and drama to get their message across.

Old Testament prophets

The Old Testament prophets were a diverse group of people whose main job was to speak God's word. They primarily addressed God's own people, to warn them or to encourage them, but they also spoke to the nations that surrounded Israel. In total, their words make up nearly one third of the Old Testament, and one fifth of the whole Bible, so their importance should not be underestimated. They were responsible for keeping people's attention focused on issues of faith, religious practice and social justice. Although there were earlier prophetic ministries, prophets were most active during a 300-year period (760–460

Prophecy location:
The major prophets are Isaiah, Jeremiah, and Ezekiel; the twelve minor prophets are Hosea, Joel, Amos, Obadiah, Jonah, Micah, Nahum, Habakkuk, Zephaniah, Haggai, Zechariah, and Malachi.

Left: Martin Luther King, Jr, speaking at a news conference in 1963.

Right: Sir Winston Churchill, British prime minister (1940–45 and 1951–55).

BC) when Israel experienced political instability and change.

There are two words used for 'prophet' in the Old Testament. The first means 'called one', indicating that the role of the prophets was really a vocation; in other words that their ministry found its origins in God's call to them. We sometimes read very specifically about this call, for example in Isaiah 6, where God's call comes to Isaiah himself. The second word means 'seer', suggesting that prophets had particular insight and could see into the future. It is only in this sense that the prophets are predictors of the future. They certainly reflected on how people's present behaviour and way of life might have future consequences, but they primarily addressed their contemporaries rather than future generations.

Over and over again, the prophets' great oracles are introduced by the phrase 'the word of the Lord came', and this is a distinguishing mark of true prophecy in the Bible. Prophets do not speak their own words, but the words of God. For this reason the prophets are to be considered as servants of God, presenting God's words and so making God and God's purposes known. Although their message was sometimes one of judgment, their purpose was always to point to the hope of restoration.

Prophets in the Old Testament

Period of prophecy	Who were the prophets of this period?	Whom did they address?	What did they say?
Early prophets	Non-writing prophets such as Elisha, Elijah, Samuel, Nathan and Gad.	Individuals, especially kings since they served in royal courts.	Gave advice relating to particular circumstances.
Eighth-century prophets	(i) Amos, Hosea (ii) Isaiah,[1] Micah	(i) Northern Kingdom (ii) Southern Kingdom	Warned that a period of security and prosperity would end because of the neglect of God's ways, but held out hope through repentance.
Prophets of the exile	(i) Jeremiah, Zephaniah, Habakkuk, Ezekiel and Obadiah (ii) Later parts of Ezekiel and Isaiah	(i) People facing uncertainty (ii) People in exile in Babylon	(i) Warned that the exile would come as a sign of God's justice. (ii) Encouraged the people that the exile would end and the result would be both physical and spiritual restoration.
Prophets after the return from exile	Haggai, Zechariah and Malachi (possibly also Joel, Jonah and Isaiah 55 onwards).	People returning to a devastated homeland.	Concerned with practical matters (for example, rebuilding the Temple) and rehabilitating people's spiritual lives. Encouraged people to believe God would intervene again in world history. More apocalyptic in character, focusing on the eternal future of God's people.

Text of Isaiah 6:1–8:

In the year that King Uzziah died, I saw the Lord seated on a throne, high and exalted, and the train of his robe filled the temple. Above him were seraphs, each with six wings: With two wings they covered their faces, with two they covered their feet, and with two they were flying. And they were calling to one another: 'Holy, holy, holy is the Lord Almighty; the whole earth is full of his glory.' At the sound of their voices the doorposts and thresholds shook and the temple was filled with smoke. 'Woe to me!' I cried. 'I am ruined! For I am a man of unclean lips, and I live among a people of unclean lips, and my eyes have seen the King, the Lord Almighty.' Then one of the seraphs flew to me with a live coal in his hand, which he had taken with tongs from the altar. With it he touched my mouth and said, 'See, this has touched your lips; your guilt is taken away and your sin atoned for.' Then I heard the voice of the Lord saying, 'Whom shall I send? And who will go for us?' And I said, 'Here am I. Send me!'

Christian people believe that Jesus is the fulfilment of the prophetic hope, but also the Word of God himself (John 1). For them Jesus is the messenger of God, as the prophets were, but he is also the message himself: this is how he fulfils the prophetic hope. His life and ministry summed up all that the prophets talked about and everything for which they longed. Jesus, like the prophets before him, made God known but, much more, he made hope and salvation attainable.

'A prophet does not speak his own words but the words of God himself.'

Poetry and song

In most English versions of the Bible it is quite straightforward to identify poetry because it is helpfully set out in lines of verse. In fact, nearly 30 per cent of the Bible is written in poetic form, and this form has many different uses, including prayers, blessings and songs of victory or praise. It is also the main form for prophetic and wisdom texts.

The purpose of poetry

But why does the Bible use poetry? Most people agree that poetry achieves different ends from narrative prose. Poetry can create humour and intensity. It can appeal to the senses and engage the imagination and the emotions. It conveys what writers felt as much as what happened to them. (The sorrow in the book of Lamentations and the joy in the Song of Songs are examples of this.) Poetry also stirs up vivid associations and is memorable. It can convey meaning that literal words might not be able to express, and in so doing it provokes a response from us. Like a musical chord, poetry can play many notes all at once and thus present the reader with challenges at more than one level. Poetry is especially apt, therefore, for describing God and God's work. God demands a response, but human language

Above: A wall painting of a musician, from the Tomb of Rekhmire, Valley of the Nobles, Thebes, Egypt.

Opposite: Prophets with scrolls are depicted in this 1139 sculpture from the doorway at Verona Cathedral.

Different types of psalms

There are 150 songs or poems contained in the book of Psalms. These are grouped into five different books (possibly to parallel the first five books of the Bible, collectively known as the Pentateuch). Within these five books, different kinds of psalms occur, each with its own mood, purpose and theme. Some of the psalms are clearly written with an individual person in mind, others are intended for corporate use by the people of God.

The psalms quickly assumed an important role in the worship life of Israel.

Augustine is depicted in mosaic in the 12th-century Palatine Chapel, Palermo, Sicily.

can never fully describe someone whose divine nature and being is beyond human comprehension.

Take, for example, probably the most famous piece of biblical poetry, Psalm 23:

The Lord is my shepherd,
I shall not be in want,
He makes me lie down in green pastures,
He leads me besides quiet waters,
He restores my soul.
He guides me in paths of righteousness for
*   his name's sake.*
Even though I walk through the valley of
*   the shadow of death,*
I will fear no evil, for you are with me;
Your rod and your staff, they comfort me.
You prepare a table before me, in the
*   presence of my enemies.*
You anoint my head with oil; my cup
*   overflows.*
Surely goodness and love will follow me all
*   the days of my life,*
And I will dwell in the house of the Lord
*   forever.*

Try putting this poem into literal language, removing all the poetic features and figurative language. What is the result? At best it would be a rather flat piece of writing, twice as long, not easily memorable and conveying a mere fraction of the intent of the original poem.

So poetry has a lot of advantages over literal language, but it also has its challenges. Poetic language is less precise, and good interpretation skills are needed to unpack its meaning. In Hebrew poetry, words can be placed in an odd order or

missed out entirely. This is particularly common in poems that are carefully structured (for example, Psalm 119, in which each stanza begins with a consecutive letter of the Hebrew alphabet). Another unusual feature of Hebrew poetry is that rhyme is not as important as parallels between lines. (Perhaps this is just as well since most of us have access to Old Testament poetry through a language other than Hebrew!) But it is worth remembering that parallelisms can serve different purposes:

◆ Sometimes the second line brings out a contrast.

◆ Sometimes the second line completes or explains an idea.

◆ Sometimes the second line repeats the same idea.

These features must be recognized if biblical poetry is to be understood correctly

in their worship of God. The hymns in the New Testament are evidence of this too (see, for example, Philippians 2:6–11; 2 Timothy 2:11–13).(See chapter 4, **Psalms** and **Wisdom**, below.)

Wisdom

The wisdom texts in the Bible find their origin in the belief that principles of wisdom that bring about harmony in the created order are inherent in the universe. This basic idea was widespread in the Ancient Near East, deriving from Egyptian and Mesopotamian writings that praised learning and science. The biblical wisdom texts discuss learning, lifestyle and worship, and commend an approach to life centred on understanding the principles of wisdom. Some of the biblical texts criticize this approach to human existence (for example, Ecclesiastes and, to some extent, Job), but in so doing they adopt the themes of the literary genre.

The wisdom texts in the Bible are grouped together because of their subject matter rather than their form. So we have a story book (Job), poetry collections (Song of Songs, Proverbs, Ecclesiastes, the wisdom Psalms) and even a New Testament letter (James), all of which could be classified as focusing on the theme of 'How to be successful in life'. These texts have different approaches and moods. Proverbs contains some light-hearted advice; Ecclesiastes is much more speculative or even cynical; James is sermon-like; and the tone of the Psalms

Poetry and song location: Found in the Psalms, the prophets and the wisdom books but also scattered in other parts of the Bible. We find examples of early Christian poetry and songs in the New Testament letters (such as Ephesians, Philippians and 2 Timothy) as well as in Revelation.

Wisdom location: Job, Song of Songs, Proverbs, Ecclesiastes, the wisdom Psalms (1, 34, 37, 49, 73, 111, 112) and possibly also the New Testament letter of James.

Illustration of King David playing the harp, from a 12th-century psalter.

and if its main ideas are to be identified. It has been suggested that understanding the poetic features of the Bible is like watching television in colour rather than black and white. St Augustine, who lived in the fifth century AD, said that the psalms helped to nurture his love for God and breathed new life into his spiritual pilgrimage. It is no wonder, then, that the psalms and other poetry in the Bible have become so well known to Christians throughout the centuries and have played an important part

Andrea del Castagno's (1421–57) depiction of James the Lesser, the writer of the New Testament letter of James.

is lyrical. But all these texts have some themes in common.

Wisdom in Proverbs

Proverbs provides a clear definition of what wisdom texts are all about in chapter 1 verses 1–7:

The proverbs of Solomon son of David, king of Israel: for attaining wisdom and discipline; for understanding words of insight; for acquiring a disciplined and prudent life, doing what is right and just and fair; for giving prudence to the simple, knowledge and discretion to the young – let the wise listen and add to their learning, and let the discerning get guidance – for understanding proverbs and parables, the sayings and riddles of the wise. The fear of the Lord is the beginning of knowledge, but fools despise wisdom and discipline.

These verses suggest that wisdom texts have a specific purpose: they increase our insight and understanding and change the way we live. They are universally applicable – to young and inexperienced people, equally to wise and discerning people. But verse 7 highlights the basic principle of all biblical wisdom texts: 'The fear of the Lord is the beginning of knowledge'. It is by fearing the Lord that success in life is secured as far as the wisdom writers are concerned. People need to choose whether to put the Lord at the centre of their lives or to follow a foolish and unsuccessful path. This idea of 'fearing the Lord' is an all-encompassing one. It includes experience and knowledge of God (Proverbs 2:5),

action (doing what is right, Proverbs 8:13) and appropriate attitudes (including humility and reverence, Proverbs 22:4). It also brings its own reward, as the poem about the successful wife at the end of Proverbs illustrates. She fears the Lord and is to be praised because her life's work (within the home and outside it), her speech and her reputation bring her the reward that 'she has earned' (Proverbs 31:31).

Wisdom and God

Although the wisdom texts are more about human life than they are about God, they do rely on the main ideas about God represented in the Bible as a whole. They speak about God as the creator who has revealed God's wisdom in God's creation. As a consequence, human life should be directed towards God, respecting the needs of other people while aiming at self-improvement. So godliness, willingness to learn, selflessness, careful speech and hard work are commended in the wisdom writings. As James writes, 'The wisdom that comes from heaven is first of all pure; then peace-loving, considerate, submissive, full of mercy and good fruit, impartial and sincere' (James 3:17). The wisdom writers urge you to live a life that recognizes God as the centre of the universe, if you want to be successful.

Letters

Twenty-one of the twenty-seven books in the New Testament are letters. Paul, the

received these letters differed in size and character, each having their own emphases, experiences and contexts. Some letters were circulars, intended for a variety of recipients. It is not surprising, therefore, that the letters in the New Testament are varied in content, length and style. Most people vary what they write and how they write it, depending on the recipient and the subject matter. Even a writer's mood, personal circumstances or available time can affect how letters are written. The New Testament letter writers were no different.

A general style of letter

There was an accepted letter-writing style in New Testament times, and most of the biblical letters follow this pattern:

- greetings (usually formal, identifying the writer first and then the intended readership);
- indication of purpose;
- main content;
- words of farewell (usually informal with personal touches).

This pattern is fairly consistent in the New Testament, although the letter to the Hebrews doesn't really have a greeting and James's letter finishes without the normal words of farewell.

The content of the letters can largely be divided into four subjects:

- Christian worship and church organization;

Letters' location:
Romans, 1 and 2 Corinthians, Galatians, Ephesians, Philippians, Colossians, 1 and 2 Thessalonians, 1 and 2 Timothy, Titus, Philemon, Hebrews, James, 1 and 2 Peter, 1, 2, and 3 John and Jude. There are also letters in the book of Revelation and within some Old Testament books (see, for example, 2 Samuel 11, 1 Kings 21, Jeremiah 29, Ezra 4).

A European renaissance painting shows Paul writing one of his letters.

founder of many New Testament churches, perhaps wrote as many as thirteen of these, while others were composed by Peter and John. As you might expect, these pieces of correspondence served very particular practical purposes. They were written in the years that followed the extraordinary events surrounding the life, death and resurrection of Jesus of Nazareth. They were sent to Christian groups and individuals who faced concerns, joys and pressures as the first believers in Jesus began to meet together. The individual recipients had their own relationships to the writers as well as their unique personalities and gifts. Likewise, the early Christian groups who

- Christian belief;

- Christian living;

- personal messages (encouragement and testimony).

Paul tends to make his sections about Christian living follow on from his sections about Christian belief. In other words he writes in a sequence that itself points out how Christian belief will always have practical implications to be worked out in life.

The occasion of letter writing

Despite similarities in form and subject matter, each letter has its own occasion.

For this reason it may be unwise to come to conclusions about church practice purely on the basis of a single section in one New Testament letter. It should be remembered, too, that reading the letters in the New Testament is sometimes like hearing one end of a telephone call: you don't always get a true impression of the whole conversation.

It is always sensible to ask why the writer wrote what he did before trying to assess what words written in one first-century letter might mean for the Christian church today. This is not to undervalue the New Testament letters, but to recognize them for what they are. They are a valuable historical witness to developing church practice and doctrine in their own times. They show Christians today that issues relating to church life and organization are not new. Although the church in its early days was not perfect, it grew and developed under the guidance of apostles who cared for it. Clearly, early on in the history of the church the central core of its message was focused on the unique life and work of Jesus and his claim on his followers' lives as they lived for him together as God's people. These New Testament letters may not give guidance to the church on every issue it faces today, but they do suggest that the presence of God will be found in the church's corporate life.

Apocalyptic literature

How they respond to political cartoons tends to divide people into two groups. Some people love them and find them easy to understand, whereas others struggle to make sense of them at all. Usually cartoons require a certain amount of knowledge about the culture in which they are set and the people they feature. Some readers immediately pick up on the sarcasm implicit in the details of the illustration, whereas others cannot see what is quite so funny or poignant.

The medium of the political cartoon is similar to the medium of apocalyptic literature in the Bible. In both there is a strong element of symbolism, and both require familiarity with their context to be properly understood.

The meaning of 'apocalyptic'

The term *apocalyptic* comes from a Greek word meaning 'to uncover' or 'to reveal', so it is clear that this form of writing, which often focuses on describing visions, is meant to clarify things for us rather than confuse us. In content, the apocalyptic writings develop the ideas of the prophets

Apocalyptic literature location: Daniel and Revelation. There are apocalyptic sections in Zechariah, Ezekiel, Isaiah and Joel, as well as in some of the literature from the period in between the Old and New Testaments.

Far left: Ruins at Corinth. Paul visited the inhabitants several times and addressed some of his letters to the Corinthians.

Top left: Stretched across wooden frames, animal skins are ready to be finished into parchment that provides a smooth writing surface. Writing materials in biblical times were prepared in a similar way.

	Prophecy	Apocalyptic literature
Occasion	760–460 BC religious crisis	200 BC – AD 200 political crisis
Form	spoken word	written
Origin	words directly from God	words from God received through angels and visions
Purpose	didactic	descriptive
Message	◆ God's justice and love ◆ need for repentance ◆ hope within history ◆ focus on the present	◆ God's eternal sovereignty ◆ need for perseverance ◆ hope outside of history ◆ focus on end times

(although there are different emphases), which explains why apocalyptic visions are found in prophetic books; both Daniel and Revelation are called prophecy and apocalypse.

This visionary literature is strongly connected to the political crises that the Jewish people and the early Christians faced when they experienced persecution. They found themselves pawns in a political game, without the power to intervene, as the Babylonians, Persians, Greeks and Romans controlled world events. It is not surprising, then, that many symbols (especially

Albrecht Dürer's (1471–1528) fantastical vision of *The Four Horsemen of the Apocalypse*.

significant colours and numbers) and cryptic expressions are used as people are encouraged to persevere, whatever the political circumstances, in the safe knowledge that God controls history from its beginning to its ultimate end.

The result of these circumstances is a type of literature that combines pessimism about the present with optimism about the long-term future. This is perhaps seen most clearly in the way that visions in Revelation are punctuated by words of blessing and hope. The literary qualities of apocalyptic texts are certainly intriguing to us today, even if, because of changing times and cultures, every detail is not fully appreciated. It is worth remembering that these visions were not meant to be analysed word for word but to paint a picture. It is certainly important to recognize that, as with political cartoons, some of the imagery is effective because it is exaggerated.

Most importantly, when we read the apocalyptic visions we should not use them as a guide to history. In fact, one of the main difficulties with apocalyptic literature is trying to work out how far in the future its point of reference is. Its purpose is clearly not to provide a historical chart about future events but to offer hope within history, on the basis of the divine control that lies outside it. It is hardly surprising, therefore, that Daniel and Revelation provide us with portraits of God (Daniel 7) as well as many titles for Jesus. Apocalyptic literature provides us with a theological mindset for surviving life, whatever it may throw at us.

Further reading suggestions

Gordon D. Fee and Douglas Stuart, *How to Read the Bible for All its Worth*, Milton Keynes: Scripture Union, 1993.

Martin Manser, *Critical Companion to the Bible*, New York: Facts on File, 2009.

Prophecy

Martin Selman, *Preaching the Prophets*, London: Spurgeon's College, 2006.

Apocalyptic literature

Jean-Pierre Prevost, *How to Read the Apocalypse*, New York: Crossroad, 1993.

Overview of the Old Testament

The Old Testament story

The Old Testament tells the story of the beginnings of human existence and of the origin and subsequent 1,000-year history of the nation of Israel. The story has a unique and specific historical and geographical setting and focuses on key episodes and people. Retelling it simply is challenging because the Old Testament presents this part of the history of civilization from the perspectives of individuals who played their own roles within it. Reading the Old Testament is like entering a national museum and seeing all its archives laid out. But, as we have noted already (see chapter 1), this diverse archive of material is presented in a story with a religious point of view. The writers record and interpret history through the lens of their faith. It is not surprising, therefore, that historical events and theological beliefs are brought together in a story which is as much a testimony to faith development as it is to history.

The beginnings of human history

The Bible starts with an account of the beginning of all things (Genesis 1–11), before the story of the Hebrew or Israelite

people really begins. These early chapters show that from the outset the story is set in a theological context affirming that the God the Israelites worship is the creator of all things. Although the world is created as perfect, sin enters the world, and along with sin comes judgment. The flood is an example of such judgment, even though God saves Noah and his family. The confusion of human languages in Genesis chapter 11 is another indication of God's judgment, and sets the scene for the call of Abraham in Genesis chapter 12.

The beginnings of a nation

The nation's beginnings are connected with one man, Abraham, whose family was associated with the Mesopotamian city of Ur (in modern Iraq). Abraham's family members were shepherds who lived a

Stained glass window depicting Adam and Eve in the Garden of Eden. It is located in Holy Trinity Cathedral, Addis Ababa and is the largest Orthodox church in Ethiopia.

A detail from *Moses Receiving the Tablets of the Law* (1960–66), by Marc Chagall.

nomadic lifestyle, and Abraham travelled with his family from Ur to Haran (in modern Turkey). Genesis 12:1–9 describes the call that Abraham received and the promise of blessing in the form of lands and nationhood. But, right from the outset, 'all people' are in view: the words of blessing to Abraham have the stated purpose of bringing blessing to everyone (Genesis 12:3). In other words, Abraham is the recipient of the blessing but also mediates it, and the former role is subservient to the latter. Abraham leads his family to Canaan, and God confirms that this is the Promised Land for his people, but although Abraham sees the land himself he does not possess it.

Abraham's immediate descendants were his son Isaac, his grandson Jacob and his great grandson Joseph (see chapter 6, **The patriarchs**). They are often referred to as the patriarchs or 'fathers' of Israel's faith. Joseph encouraged his family to leave Canaan and live in Egypt at a time of widespread famine. However, the pharaohs of Egypt ended up treating the Hebrew people as slaves, and Moses – an Israelite who had received an Egyptian upbringing and education – led a group of them into the Sinai desert to escape. It was at this time that Moses encountered the God whom Abraham had met and trusted. Moses accepted that it was his task to lead God's people in God's way. He received the Ten Commandments on Mount Sinai as regulations to help the Israelites live as the covenant (see chapter 2, **Covenant**) people of God, as well as detailed instructions for building a tabernacle (see glossary) and worshipping God. Moses and the people left Mount Sinai and continued their nomadic wandering in the desert until Moses died. Joshua then took up the leadership and led the people across the River Jordan into the land of Canaan. The Israelites experienced a number of spectacular victories over the Canaanite (see chapter 7, **Canaanites**) peoples.

The nation has a land

Despite the fact that the Israelites occupied a large area of land, mainly west of the Jordan, the original Canaanite clans were never totally ousted from Canaan, and this proved to be a permanent problem for the Israelites. Furthermore, as the Israelites were thinking about extending the area they occupied, so were other groups, such as the forceful Philistines (see chapter 7, **Philistines**). Leaders among the Israelites, such as Deborah, Samson, Gideon and Samuel, were very concerned at the religious consequences of mixing with these groups. People were tempted to make alliances with them, and even to worship their gods, rather than believe that the God whom their fathers had trusted would continue to protect them even in these volatile times.

Eventually the Israelite people decided that they should at least have the same form of government as other nations, so they appointed their first king, King Saul. The accounts of Israel's kings in the Old Testament do not shy away from describing the weaknesses as well as the strengths of Israel's leaders.

The Israelites have a king

Saul was set apart as king by Samuel the prophet. He became known for his military prowess, although he was never able to overcome the Philistines, and religious matters did not seem to be high on his agenda. The defeat of Goliath, a Philistine giant and champion, by a young boy called David eventually led to Saul's political downfall and David's appointment as king.

David received a promise of God's presence and blessing, just as Abraham had, when he took up his position as ruler over the Israelites. Although David made mistakes, his military campaigns against the Philistines were very successful and he began to establish Jerusalem as the centre of both political power and religious worship, housing there the **Ark of the Covenant** (see glossary). From this point on Jerusalem became God's city, and the building of the Temple dominated Israel's religious history. David died in old age, to be replaced by his son Solomon. Together

David and Solomon represent the golden age of Israel's national history, before more troubled times began.

Solomon's contribution to Israel's history is strongly identified with the fact that he built the Temple in Jerusalem, making it the permanent centre of religious and political life for the Israelites. Solomon was also celebrated as a king of wisdom and riches. However, there was always rebellion among his followers, and gradually opponents appeared. Solomon's reign lasted for forty years, and after it the people of Israel divided into two.

Detail showing David beheading Goliath with his own sword, from the Gates of Paradise in Florence, Italy, by Lorenzo Ghiberti (1378–1455).

The Israelites divide

Solomon was succeeded by his son, Rehoboam, but only the tribe of Judah, to which Rehoboam belonged, followed his leadership. This single tribe became the state of Judah, ruled by kings whose line of succession went back to King David and occupying the south of the territory. In the north the other tribes established themselves as the state of Israel.

Without a historical line of succession, Israel struggled from the outset. Its 200-year history is littered with uprisings and assassinations, despite the emergence of Samaria as its capital city. It had a precarious geographical position, always susceptible to attacks from surrounding peoples. The prophet Elijah (see chapter 6) was one of many who warned Israel about its moral decline in being drawn away from its covenant commitment, and its political insecurity. As the Assyrians (see chapter 7) advanced, other prophets such as Hosea and Micah told Israel that its only hope was to return to God – otherwise its moral decline would destroy it. When the capital city fell to the Assyrians, the tribes in Israel were deported and dispersed, and their land was quickly taken over by other people.

Judah was more stable and less troubled. The line of succession back to David ensured a smooth handover of power, and the country's small size and geographical position meant it was of less interest to the military and political powers that surrounded it. Although prophets such as Isaiah, Micah and Jeremiah warned Judah against religious complacency, its capital, Jerusalem, with its Temple, still served as a symbol of its religious commitment. However, some people in

A 7th-century BC Assyrian relief of soldiers from Persepolis.

Map showing the division of the kingdom into Israel (north) and Judah (south)

Judah considered themselves immune to both God's judgment on their behaviour and the threat posed by other nations. In the end, despite surviving threats from Syria and Assyria, Judah fell to the power of the Babylonian empire (see chapter 7), resulting in the fall of Jerusalem, the destruction of the Temple and the nation's demise.

The nation in exile

The Babylonians took the leaders of Judah into captivity and left the rest of the people without government and security in a ruined land. Many of them left Judah in search of a better life, and new ways of maintaining Israelite faith and belief emerged. Prophets such as Jeremiah and Ezekiel continued to reassure the people that God's commitment to them as a nation meant they had a future and a hope because God would restore their fortunes. The exile (see glossary) lasted about fifty years and only ended when the Babylonians themselves were overthrown by the newly emerging Persian empire, led by Cyrus. Cyrus allowed the exiles to return home.

The nation re-emerges

It seems as though some Jews had become accustomed to the Babylonian way of life and did not see much reason to return to Palestine. Eventually prophets such as Ezra and Nehemiah successfully encouraged the people to return in order to rebuild the Temple in Jerusalem, which was viewed as a symbol of the political and religious re-emergence of the Jewish people.

In this period the people began to show a new interest in their religious life and faith, having been encouraged by the events of Cyrus's conquest to believe that God still had a future for them. In the minds of many Jews, however, the period of exile never fully came to an end, and the pain of this dominated Jewish consciousness even in New Testament times.

During the final part of the history covered by the Old Testament, tensions with surrounding nations and with the remnants of the other tribes of Israel remained – tensions which explain the animosity, for example, between Jews and Samaritans in New Testament times. The Jews faced other threats, too, as the Greeks and Romans emerged as world powers. However, Jewish people view their history as a testimony to God's presence with and promise to them. It is as such a 'Testament' that the story of the nation of Israel has worth and relevance to Christians as well as Jews today.

The Old Testament story of history and faith

Time-line	Episodes in Israel's history	Themes	Historical sources	Prophetic ministries
2000 BC	**The beginnings of a nation**	God calls individuals to lead the people, and promises nationhood	Genesis, Exodus, Leviticus, Numbers, Deuteronomy	
Patriarchal period 1800 BC onwards	Patriarchs: Abraham to Joseph			
1705 BC To Egypt				
c. 1350–1300 BC Moses				
1275 BC Escape from Egypt	Exodus under Moses	God makes a covenant with the people as a whole		
1220 BC Entry into Canaan under Joshua	**The nation has a land**	The land is the promise of God realized	Joshua, Judges	
Period of judges		God is Israel's king		
Samuel's ministry begins				
1030–1010 BC Saul	**The Israelites have a king**	Allegiance to the God of the covenant is vital	1 and 2 Samuel, 1 and 2 Kings, 1 and 2 Chronicles	The early prophets: Samuel, Nathan, and Gad
1010–970 BC David 1000 BC David takes control of Jerusalem		Kings are the servants of God		
970–931 BC Solomon				
920 BC The nation divides into north and south kingdoms	**The Israelites divide**	Trust in God alone	1 and 2 Samuel, 1 and 2 Kings, 1 and 2 Chronicles	The eighth-century prophets: Isaiah, Amos, Hosea and Micah
883 BC Assyrian power re-emerges				
753 BC Rome is founded				

Time-line	Episodes in Israel's history	Themes	Historical sources	Prophetic ministries
722 BC Fall of Samaria 587 BC Fall of Jerusalem	Israel defeated by the Assyrians Judah defeated by the Babylonians	Sin brings consequences	1 and 2 Samuel, 1 and 2 Kings, 1 and 2 Chronicles	The immediate pre-exilic prophets: Nahum, Habakkuk, Zephaniah and Ezekiel
586 BC Exile 539 BC Babylonia conquered by the Persians	The nation in exile	Israel's punishment is permitted by God. Hope is based on God's promise and his love for his people		The exilic prophets: Isaiah (40ff.), Ezekiel and Obadiah
538 BC Edict of Cyrus 537 BC The foundations of the second Temple are laid 520–515 BC the second Temple is built 499 BC War between Greece and Persia 336–323 BC Reign of Alexander the Great	The nation re-emerges Gradual return of the Jews to Palestine The Temple is rebuilt	Worship becomes central to Israel's life	Ezra to Nehemiah	The post-exilic prophets: Haggai, Malachi and Zechariah

The Old Testament books

Genesis
'In the beginning...'

Theme: Genesis is a book about the beginnings of the world, the human race and the nation of Israel. It shows how God can bring new beginnings whatever the circumstances – from chaos (in nature), from sinfulness (in the human race), from barrenness (in Abraham's family). By God's word, God creates the world and calls people to play their part in God's purposes. God provides for the people, promising that they will have their own land. God is also just and holy and responds to wrongdoing with forms of punishment (such as the flood) which protect God's creation and people.

Well-known passages:
1 the creation of the world
2–3 Adam and Eve
6 Noah and the flood
11 the Tower of Babel
12 the call of Abraham
22 the test of Abraham's faith
37–40 Joseph's dreams
41 Joseph interprets Pharaoh's dreams

Main characters: Adam and Eve, Cain and Abel, Noah, the patriarchs and their families – Abraham and Sarah, Isaac and Rebekah, Esau (and his Canaanite wives), Jacob, Leah and Rachel, and the twelve sons of Jacob, including Joseph.

Exodus
'You will know that I am the Lord your God.'

Theme: the title of Exodus means 'way out' or 'exit' and the book relates how the people of Israel escape from slavery in Egypt about 400 years after Joseph's death. When they leave Egypt they are without a home and wander in the desert for many years. First, God persuades Moses to lead the people, reaffirming the promises made to Abraham; then God tells the people how they are to live. Being God's people involves privileges and responsibilities, agreed in a covenant of loyalty. God provides them with a leader, a promise, deliverance from Egypt and food in the desert. Most of all God assures them of God's love. The purpose of their freedom is that they should trust God, know God's presence and worship God, hence the detailed instructions about worship in this book.

Main characters: Moses, Aaron and Pharaoh.

The Ten Commandments

Otherwise known collectively as the 'Decalogue' (the 'ten words'), the Ten Commandments outline the regulations that will preserve the relationship between God and God's people established by the covenant. These words are spoken to God's people after they have been led out of Egypt. The commandments regulate life so that God's honour and the people's well-being are preserved, and they live as faithful people. The commandments are found twice in the Bible: in Exodus 20:2–17 and Deuteronomy 5:6–21. There are slight variations between these two texts. One such variation is in the reason for resting on the sabbath. In Exodus the reason given relates to God's own sabbath rest after the creation of the world; in Deuteronomy, it is based on remembering the experience of slavery in Egypt. Some explanation can be provided for this variation: Exodus commonly has a universal perspective (remember that the whole world is created by God), whereas Deuteronomy's focus is often more Israelite-specific (look back at your own history as a people). (See chapter 3, **Law**, chapter 9 panel: **Who is God; What is God like?**)

Well-known passages:
3 Moses and the burning bush
7–11 the ten plagues of Egypt
12 the first Passover
13 crossing of the Red Sea
16 God gives the people manna
20 the Ten Commandments
25 the Ark of the Covenant
32 Aaron and the golden calf

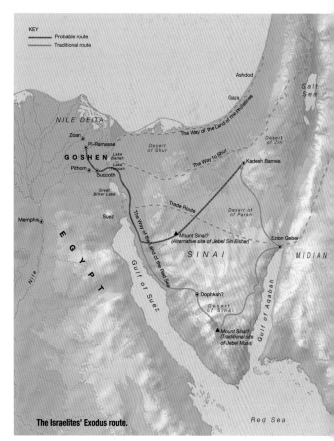

The Israelites' Exodus route.

Left: The Parting of the Red Sea, as illustrated by Becquet in an 18th-century French catechism.

Numbers

Theme: Numbers continues the story of the exodus from the point when the people leave their encampment in the desert until the land of Canaan comes into view. During this time the people grumble that life in the desert is no better than the life they left behind in Egypt. The book contains a head-count of those who have left Egypt, a family-count of the Levite tribes and census details of the people who travel. Commandments relating to purity are reiterated and the challenges of the journey towards Canaan are recorded, including opposition from within the people of Israel and from surrounding peoples.

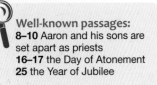

Well-known passages:
9 the cloud above the tabernacle leads the people
11 God provides quail as food for a complaining people
13 spies are sent to Canaan
22 Balaam and the talking donkey

Main characters: Moses and Aaron.

Leviticus
'Be holy, because I am holy.'

Theme: as the title indicates, Leviticus is an instruction book for the priests from the tribe of Levi, who are charged with advising God's people on how they should live and worship. The priests are responsible for caring for the tabernacle, but the instructions here cover many aspects of life, including food, health, family and social relationships, civil law and religious practice. God's holiness means that God's people must lead holy lives, but the laws protect and help the people as well as safeguard their covenant relationship with God.

Well-known passages:
8–10 Aaron and his sons are set apart as priests
16–17 the Day of Atonement
25 the Year of Jubilee

Main characters: Moses, Aaron and the priests.

Deuteronomy

'The Lord your God has chosen you... because he loved you.'

Theme: the title of Deuteronomy means 'second law' but, rather than being a new law, Deuteronomy presents a copy or repetition of the laws of Sinai. Most of the book consists of the persuasive words of Moses to God's people. It is frequently quoted in the New Testament and takes as its theme the encompassing love of God for the chosen people. The laws are restated because by keeping them God's people will be blessed in the land that they will enter.

Well-known passages:
5 the Ten Commandments
6 the Jewish *Shema* (verses 4–5)
27–28 curses and blessings from Mount Ebal
32–34 Moses' farewell song and his death

The *Shema* (Hebrew word meaning 'Hear') is one of the most important Jewish prayers. Children learn it at an early age. Jews repeat this prayer three times a day as part of their regular devotions. Most synagogue services include it.

Main characters: Moses and Aaron.

Joshua

Theme: Joshua, Moses' successor, leads the people into the Promised Land (Canaan) and they gradually take it over. The people assign various territories to each of the tribes. One of Joshua's final acts is to lead the people in an act of worship to renew the covenant. Possessing this land establishes Israel as a people with a future. They are always to remember that the land was God's gift to them.

Well-known passages:
2 two Israelite spies are protected by Rahab
3–4 the Israelites cross the Jordan
6 the walls of Jericho fall down
10 the sun stands still

Main character: Joshua.

Top left: A 1705 etching by of the twelve tribes of Judea encamped around the Tabernacle in the desert. Artist unknown.

Left: The consecration of Eleazar (son of Aaron) as high priest by Moses and Aaron, as told in Numbers 20:25–27. Illustration by William Hole 1846–1917.

Right: Joshua urges on his army outside the walls of Jericho. Trumpeters process around the walls carrying the Ark of the Covenant and the walls crumble. Illustration from a late 19th-century Bible.

Judges

'The Lord raised up judges who saved them.'

Theme: after Joshua's death, 'judges' take charge of the tribes in Canaan and experience success in battle. However, the people ignore God's laws and are tempted to turn to the gods worshipped by the nations around them. The book portrays God's people as rebellious, but God wants to help them even though God is displeased with them. God punishes them in order to restore and renew them. The result is a cycle of sin followed by forgiveness. God's Spirit is at work in individuals' lives during this period of unsettled history.

Well-known passages:
5 the Song of Deborah
7 Gideon selects a small number of men to defeat the Midianites
13 the birth of Samson
16 Samson and Delilah

Main characters: the judges (Deborah, Gideon, Jephthah and Samson).

Ruth

'Your people will be my people and your God my God.'

Theme: set in the unsettled period of the judges, the story of Ruth is testimony to the faith of one family. Ruth is a widowed Moabite woman who is wholly committed to the God of the Israelites. In her destitution she follows her mother-in-law Naomi, back to Bethlehem and marries Boaz, a wealthy landowner. The story is about human and divine loving-kindness and faithfulness. It is also significant that Ruth is a Moabite, and she gives birth to Obed whose descendants include King David.

Well-known passages:
1:16–18 Ruth's words of commitment to Naomi and her God
4 Ruth and Boaz marry

Main characters: Ruth, Naomi and Boaz.

1 Samuel

Theme: 1 Samuel begins with an account of Samuel's birth, childhood and early prophetic ministry (mainly concerned with urging Israel to put God first again). It is Samuel who anoints Israel's first king, Saul, with whom the era of the judges comes to an end as monarchy is established. Saul does not listen to God's word as declared by Samuel and God rejects Saul as king. Eventually David emerges as a promising future king, but Saul is very envious of this young upstart and his popularity. As David rises Saul falls and, having been critically wounded in a battle against the Philistines, Saul takes his own life.

Well-known passages:
3 Samuel, as a child with Eli in the Temple, hears God's call
16:1–13 Samuel anoints David
16:14–23 David plays the harp for Saul
17 David kills Goliath the giant
20 the friendship between David and Jonathan

Main characters: Samuel, Eli, Hannah, Saul, Jonathan and David.

2 Samuel

'[David], your house and your kingdom shall endure forever before me, your throne shall be established forever.'

Theme: David succeeds Saul as king and acts as both a military and a religious leader, bringing some unity between the tribes of Israel and restoring the Ark to its central place in Jerusalem, the capital city and royal residence. David achieves military success and is rewarded as God makes a special covenant with him that his family line will last forever. Even though David is guilty of great sins (including adultery and murder), the promise is not revoked, although David is not allowed to build the Temple. David is aware that God has been merciful to him and his family, and responds with a song of praise that reflects sentiments in the Psalms.

Well-known passages:
6 the Ark comes to Jerusalem
7 God's covenant with David
11 David's affair with Bathsheba

Main characters: David, Nathan and Absalom.

Far left: Samson and Delilah, 1851, by José Pina (1830–1909).

Bottom left: Ruth entreats Naomi to allow her to stay (Ruth 1:16): wood engraving after Gustave Doré.

Above: Saul is anointed by Samuel (1 Samuel 10:1), c. 1860; artist unknown.

is weak and splits into two halves under the rule of Rehoboam (Judah) and Jeroboam (Israel). After Solomon, prophets including Elisha and Elijah bring God's message to the people. The low point of this period is the reign in Israel of the evil King Ahab. Kings are assessed for their religious impact more than for their political or military abilities.

Main characters: Solomon, Elisha, Elijah and Ahab.

2 Kings

Theme: 2 Kings continues the account of the history of the kings of Judah and Israel, and ends by describing the events surrounding the downfall of Israel and the fall of Jerusalem, leading to the Babylonian exile. Hezekiah outlaws idol worship, and Josiah reminds the people of God's laws, but the people of God nevertheless experience spiritual and physical decline, despite the continued prophetic ministries of Elijah and Elisha.

Main characters: Elijah, Elisha, Ahaz, Hezekiah and Josiah.

1 Kings

Well-known passages:
3 Solomon's wisdom
6 description of Solomon's Temple
10 the Queen of Sheba visits Solomon
17 ravens feed Elijah
18 the contest between the prophets of the Lord and the prophets of Baal

'Your hearts must be fully committed to the Lord our God.'

Theme: 1 and 2 Kings cover the history of the monarchy from the reign of Solomon, David's son and successor, to the fall of the monarchy in Judah at the hands of the Babylonians. Solomon's reign is dominated by building the Temple in Jerusalem, and his wisdom and wealth are celebrated. But Solomon is not loyal to God and by the time he dies the kingdom

Well-known passages:
4 Elisha's miracles (the widow's oil, the Shunammite son)
5 Naaman is healed of leprosy
23 Josiah renews the covenant
25 the fall of Jerusalem

1 Chronicles

Theme: although they cover the same history as the preceding four books, 1 and 2 Chronicles were written much later (after the exile) and emphasize that God intends what happens for the good of the people, whom God will restore. Genealogies play an important part in tracing the history of God's people. There is a special focus on the worship life of Israel, which places the Temple and the role of the priests at the heart of these stories.

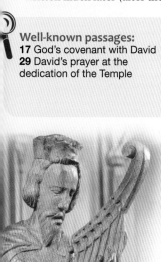

Well-known passages:
17 God's covenant with David
29 David's prayer at the dedication of the Temple

Main characters: David and Solomon.

2 Chronicles

'If my people who are called by my name will humble themselves and pray and seek my face and turn from their wicked ways then will I hear from heaven and will forgive their sin and will heal their land.'

Well-known passages:
1 Solomon asks for wisdom
7 God's words to Solomon at the dedication of the Temple
33 the repentance of King Manasseh
34 Josiah finds the Book of the Law
36 the fall of Jerusalem

Theme: The book of 2 Chronicles continues to revisit the history of the monarchy following David's death, emphasizing the centrality of the Temple for God's people (chapters 1–9), although the book ends with the tragedy of the Temple's destruction (chapter 36). The Southern Kingdom of Judah receives all the attention, indicating that for the Chronicler the hope for God's people is to be found with the royal line of David (whatever the shortcomings of individual kings). After the exile, God's people will be restored and signs of that restoration are already apparent in the history of Judah.

Main characters: Solomon, David, Hezekiah, Josiah and the kings of Judah.

Top left: Detail from the Ishtar Gate, Babylon.

Left: King David statue from the 13th-century Bamberg Cathedral in Germany.

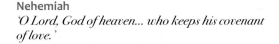

Ezra

Theme: the book of Ezra describes the return from exile, the rebuilding of the Temple, Ezra's own return to Jerusalem and the reforms he instigated.

Well-known passages:
1 Cyrus allows the Jews to return from exile
6 the Temple is rebuilt and the first Passover is celebrated
9 Ezra's prayer of confession

The books of Ezra and Nehemiah have historical and theological similarities to 1 and 2 Chronicles. A special feature of Ezra is the prominent place given to official letters, often recorded in the Aramaic language. The book is set after Cyrus the Persian ruler has subdued the Babylonians, and God's people begin to return from exile.

Main characters: Cyrus, Zerubbabel, Jeshua, Darius I, Artaxerxes and Ezra.

Nehemiah

'O Lord, God of heaven... who keeps his covenant of love.'

Theme: whereas Ezra is primarily concerned with the rebuilding of the Temple, Nehemiah focuses on the rebuilding of the walls of Jerusalem. This is a community effort and, despite opposition, is achieved in less than two months. The book describes Nehemiah's return from exile and his management of the rebuilding project, emphasizing too the religious reforms overseen by him and by Ezra.

Main characters: Nehemiah and Ezra.

Well-known passages:
1 Nehemiah's prayer of confession
8 Ezra reads the law
9 the people's prayer of confession

Left: King Cyrus II of Persia restores the sacred vessels and releases the captive Jewish people. From a reproduction of an illustration by Gustave Doré.

Top right: Students gather around Rabbi Svei at an Orthodox Jewish yeshiva in Philadelphia on Purim. One student wears a mock beard on the one day that such humour is allowed.

Esther

Theme: the story of Esther follows the life events of a young Jewish orphan girl who rises from obscurity to become queen consort to the Persian king Xerxes. Although a queen, Esther is at the mercy of a volatile king, and it takes courage and planning to defeat the evil plan of Haman, one of the king's advisors, who seeks to kill all the Jewish people in the Persian empire. The story is testimony to God's protecting the people, even though God is not mentioned in the story. Jews continue to celebrate their extraordinary preservation through the annual carnival celebration of Purim (see glossary). At this festival Jewish children re-enact the story: Haman is booed as the villain and Esther cheered as the heroine.

Well-known passages:
2 Esther is taken to the harem and emerges as queen
4 Esther accepts her role to help her people
7 Haman is hanged
9 the celebration of Purim

Main characters: Xerxes, Haman, Mordecai and Esther.

Job

'I know that my redeemer lives. The Lord gave and the Lord has taken away; may the name of the Lord be praised.'

Theme: this story concerns a righteous man who loses everything that matters to him – his health, his property and his family – and struggles to relate his suffering to his faith in God. Satan's involvement is revealed at the outset. Job's friends Eliphaz, Bildad and Zophar offer him various ways of interpreting his experience. In the end suffering brings Job closer to God, and he affirms that God's ways are beyond human understanding. The benefits of Job's former life are restored and, in fact, 'the Lord blessed the latter part of his life more than the former'. The story's message is less an answer to why people suffer than a reflection on how people should endure suffering in humble reliance upon God.

Well-known passages:
1 Satan talks with God
23 Job tells his friends that God seems absent
38 God speaks to Job
42 Job acknowledges that God's ways are wonderful

Main characters: Job, Eliphaz, Bildad and Zophar.

Psalms

Theme: Psalms is a collection of poems that serve as prayers and hymns in Israelite worship. Many are ascribed to King David, but the final collection has been gathered and organized over a long period of time. The style and structure of the psalms is varied, but they all help to show how God's people pray (please... help... sorry) and praise God. The prayers are honest writings expressing a range of human emotions within the context of trusting that God will respond to heartfelt prayers. The psalms illustrate that prayer and praise cannot be separated.

Well-known passages:
1 'Blessed is the one who...'
8 'O Lord, our Lord, how majestic is your name in all the earth!'
19 'The heavens declare the glory of God'
23 'The Lord is my shepherd'
46 'God is our refuge and strength'
51 'Have mercy on me, O God'
93 'The Lord reigns'
100 'Shout for joy to the Lord'
119 in praise of God's law
121 'I lift my eyes to the hills'
136 'Give thanks to the Lord... His love endures forever'
139 'O Lord, you have searched me...'
150 'Let everything that has breath praise the Lord'

Right: King Solomon writing Proverbs. Engraving by Gustave Doré (1832–83).

Far right: Depiction of the prophet Isaiah in a stained glass window, Leek, Staffordshire, UK

Proverbs
'The fear of the Lord is the beginning of wisdom.'

Theme: the book of Proverbs contains mainly short statements about the way life works and how we should live. They focus on what it means to be wise and to fear (that is to respect) God. In chapter 1, verses 1–7 provide a summary of the purpose of the book of Proverbs and the final verses contain an example of what a wise life looks like (the wise wife, 31:10–31). Chapter 8 is significant because it offers a figurative description of wisdom. The book provides common-sense advice, but always in a religious framework that presents life as a blessing and gift from God.

Well-known passages:
3:5–6 'Trust in the Lord with all your heart...'
6:6 'Go to the ant, you sluggard; consider its ways and be wise'
11:22 'Like a gold ring in a pig's snout is a beautiful woman who shows no discretion'
17:1 'Better a dry crust with peace and quiet than a house full of feasting with strife'
17:12 'Better to meet a bear robbed of her cubs than a fool in his folly'
21:9 'Better to live on the corner of a roof than share a house with a quarrelsome wife'
27:6 'Wounds from a friend can be trusted, but an enemy multiplies kisses'

Ecclesiastes

Theme: the origin, author, date and purpose of Ecclesiastes remain uncertain. What is clear is that this is a reflection on life and experience which is realistic, even cynical, and leads to the conclusion that God remains the interpretative key to life. (The Hebrew title for this book simply means 'teacher'; the Greek title, 'Ecclesiastes', refers to an assembly, possibly implying that these are words addressed to a large group.)

Well-known passages:
1 Everything is meaningless: 'there is nothing new under the sun'
3 a time for everything: 'a time to be born and a time to die'
12 'Remember your Creator in the days of your youth'

Song of Songs

'Many waters cannot quench love.'

Well-known passage:
2:16 'My lover is mine and I am his'

Theme: a series of love songs and poems (possibly by King Solomon but more likely composed in the period after the exile) depict the intensity of human passion and emotion in the relationship between a man and a woman. Although sometimes explained as describing God's love for us, this book is primarily about celebrating the human experience of love; like all human experiences, however, this love finds its source in our status as created beings in God's image.

Main characters: the lover and the loved one.

Isaiah

Theme: Isaiah is often called 'the evangelical prophet'. Certainly the prophecies, usually understood as originating from a lengthy period of Israel's history, present the good news that God is creator and saviour of Israel and all nations. These prophecies are defiantly monotheistic and in places satirize the numerous deities of surrounding nations (see especially chapters 40 and 46). The book contains many prophecies about the restoration of Israel, the judgment on other nations and the future worship of Israel's God by other nations. There is a special focus on the 'servant of the Lord' who will bring justice and peace among the nations. Christians view the 'Servant Songs' as anticipatory celebrations of the saving work of Jesus Christ.

Well-known passages:
6 the call of Isaiah
7 Immanuel's birth
9 the prediction of a child's birth: 'For to us a child is born'
11 the description of the messianic age
42:1–4; 49:1–6; 50:4–9; 52:13 – 53:12 the Servant Songs
61 words Jesus applied to himself while preaching in Nazareth (see Luke 4:16–21)

Main character: Isaiah.

Jeremiah

Theme: the prophet Jeremiah warns the people of Judah (from Josiah's time until the exile) that following false gods and false prophets will have serious consequences. Jeremiah combines this note of impending judgment with optimism and hope based on God's eternal love for his people. He tells them that the exile will take place but that God will restore them. Jeremiah's own life was not an easy one but he served God faithfully despite opposition and inner struggles.

Well-known passages:
1 Jeremiah's call
18–19 Jeremiah at the potter's house
31 the new covenant written on hearts
37 Jeremiah is imprisoned

Main character: Jeremiah.

Lamentations

Theme: the book of Lamentations is a series of poems lamenting the fall of Jerusalem and the subsequent exile of God's people. Sometimes Jeremiah is identified as the author of these poems, as they reflect elements of the style and subject matter of Jeremiah's prophecies. The personal, social and religious consequences of exile are described vividly, but God is still in control and will forgive God's people. Again despair meets hope.

Well-known passages:
3:26 'It is good to wait patiently for the salvation of the Lord'
3:23 'Great is your faithfulness'
5:21 'Restore us to yourself, O Lord, that we may return'

Ezekiel

'Dry bones hear the word of the Lord... I will put breath into you and you will come to life.'

Theme: in unsettled days when the Assyrians, Babylonians, Egyptians and Persians were exerting their military strength, the prophet Ezekiel, one of the exiled Jewish community in Babylon, used drama and symbolism to underline the importance of his message. Like Jeremiah, he experienced personal trials; but he delivered a message of hope to a suffering people based on God's work of restoration. Ezekiel is keen to point out that though community is important, individuals must take responsibility for their own response to God's word. The book concludes with a detailed description of Ezekiel's vision of a new Temple.

Well-known passages:
1 Ezekiel's vision of God
3–4 two prophetic dramas: eating a scroll and laying on his side
34 God is the shepherd of his people
36 God promises a new heart and a new spirit
37 the valley of dry bones

Daniel

Theme: Daniel lives among the exiled community in Babylon but is in training for service in the royal court of Nebuchadnezzar, along with his fellow-Israelites Shadrach, Meshach and Abednego. Chapters 1–6 describe Daniel's faith and uncompromising loyalty to the God of Israel, even when he is thrown into a

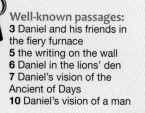

Well-known passages:
3 Daniel and his friends in the fiery furnace
5 the writing on the wall
6 Daniel in the lions' den
7 Daniel's vision of the Ancient of Days
10 Daniel's vision of a man

fiery furnace for not bowing to Nebuchadnezzar's image. Belshazzar and then Darius[1] succeed Nebuchadnezzar, and Daniel rises to favour. Envious of Daniel, some royal officials have him thrown to the lions for praying to God. Daniel's miraculous survival causes Darius to acknowledge Daniel's God as the living God. Chapters 7 onwards present Daniel's apocalyptic visions, some of which Christians interpret as signs of the messianic age inaugurated in Jesus.

Main characters: Daniel, Shadrach, Meshach, Abednego and Nebuchadnezzar.

Hosea

'I will heal their waywardness and love them freely.'

Theme: Hosea's ministry is set in the last days of the Northern Kingdom before Israel finally fell to the Assyrians. The book is divided into two related parts: chapters 1–3 describe Hosea's decision to obey God's command to love his adulterous wife; chapters 4–14 record Hosea's prophetic message to God's people that they need to repent and turn back to God, and then God will forgive them and show God's love to them. The interplay between faithfulness and faithlessness is present throughout, with emphasis on the love of the faithful partner. Hosea reassures the people that God is loyal to them because the covenant depends on God's eternal love. Hosea is the first of the twelve minor prophetic books sometimes referred to collectively as 'The Book of the Twelve'.

Well-known passages:
3 God tells Hosea to love his adulterous wife again
6:6 'I desire mercy, not sacrifice'
11 God's love for Israel

Main characters: Hosea and his wife Gomer.

Left: Late 19th-century illustration depicting Ezekiel's vision of the restoration of the Temple (Ezekiel 47).

Above: Roman mosaic showing Daniel having been cast into the Lions' den by Darius, king of Babylon.

Joel

Theme: with no historical references, this book is difficult to date, but its prophecies anticipate a coming day of the Lord (see glossary) which will bring judgment to unfaithful Israel before blessing and restoration, including the gift of God's Spirit.

Well-known passage:
2:28 God will pour out his Spirit on the Day of the Lord (see glossary) (see Acts 2:1–33)

Amos

'Hate evil, love good; maintain justice in the courts.'

Well-known passages:
5 call to repentance
6 complacent and proud people will be exiled
9 Israel will be destroyed but then restored

Theme: the shepherd-prophet Amos brings messages from God to both parts of the divided kingdom during a period of political stability but religious corruption. The neglect of social justice and the exploitation of the poor concern Amos. God's people can expect punishment because God's righteous justice demands it. However, God is also majestic and merciful, so there is hope for the people.

Obadiah

Theme: Obadiah contains a short prophecy (difficult to date) against Edom (the descendants of Esau), who were enemies of God's people at various points in their history.

Jonah

Theme: a prophet called Jonah is sent to Nineveh but runs away instead. God intervenes, causing Jonah to be swallowed by a huge fish and to remain inside it for three days, and Jonah decides he should go to Nineveh after all. Jonah's message is that the people in Nineveh need to repent of their wickedness. God surprises even Jonah by the extent of his mercy and compassion to repentant people. Unlike other prophetic books Jonah is not written in poetry but prose narrative.

Main character: Jonah.

Well-known passages:
1 Jonah is swallowed by a great fish
3 'Who knows? God may yet relent and with compassion turn from his fierce anger'

Micah

'But you, Bethlehem Ephrathah... out of you will come for me one who will be ruler over Israel, whose origins are from of old, from ancient times.'

Well-known passages:
4 peace in Jerusalem, 'swords into ploughshares'
5:2 a promised ruler from Bethlehem
6:6–8 God requires justice and mercy

Theme: Micah's prophecies reflect an eighth-century BC setting and address many of the issues relating to social justice also present in Amos. The message of hope and salvation is interspersed with messages of judgment. Micah anticipates a time when God's glory and past blessings on Jerusalem will be superseded in a new age, when a ruler will come from Bethlehem to establish peace and security once more.

Nahum

'The Lord is slow to anger and great in power; the Lord will not leave the guilty unpunished.'

Theme: Nahum speaks about God's coming judgment on wickedness before the downfall of Nineveh in 612 BC. The prophecies reveal that God's mercy is not compromised by his acts of judgment against wickedness. God is sovereign over all nations. The prophecies are rhetorical poems full of powerful imagery.

Habakkuk

Theme: sometimes called the complaining prophet, Habakkuk wrestles with questions about how God's plans don't meet his expectations. God plans to use the Babylonians to punish the people of Judah, and Habakkuk can't understand this. But he is convinced that God is just and in control of all history so the book ends with a confident statement of trust.

Well-known passages:
2:4 'The righteous will live by their faith'
3 Habakkuk's prayer: 'In wrath remember mercy'

Far left: Shepherds with their flocks in the Jordan Valley.

Left: Historiated initial E depicting Jonah being thrown into the sea from the Souvigny Bible, late 12th century.

Zephaniah

Theme: active during the early days of Josiah's reign, Zephaniah announces that God's judgment against Judah is on its way. Amid this solemn message, there is hope that God will act to restore the people's fortunes.

Well-known passage:
3:17 Jerusalem's future: 'The Lord your God is with you, he is mighty to save…'

Haggai

Theme: the prophecies of Haggai promise the returned exiles that they will be given the help of the Spirit of God as they rebuild the Temple walls. They can anticipate God's help, spiritual restoration and blessing.

Main characters: Haggai and Zerubbabel.

Well-known passage:
2:9 'The glory of this present house will be greater than the glory of the former house'

Zechariah

Theme: like Haggai, Zechariah urges the returned community to rebuild the Temple. He reminds the people that their lives must match the glory that is theirs as God's people. Zechariah's prophecies use symbolic language to describe apocalyptic visions which anticipate the end times and urge God's people to put him first.

Well-known passages:
4:6 'Not by might, nor by power, but by my Spirit says the Lord Almighty'
9 the coming king: 'gentle and riding on a donkey'
11:12 'thirty pieces of silver'
12:10–12 weeping in Jerusalem for 'the one they have pierced'
13:1 a fountain to cleanse Jerusalem from sin

Main characters: Zechariah, Joshua, Zerubbabel.

In Zechariah 11:12–13, the people value the shepherd at the price of 30 pieces of silver. See also Matthew 26:15.

Malachi

' *"I have loved you, says the Lord. I the Lord do not change." '

Theme: some time after the Temple is rebuilt, this prophet reminds God's people that God does not change. God's love is faithful and God's promises will be fulfilled. God's purposes will be seen and the people need to live justly and worship God with integrity.

Well-known passages:
2:16 "I hate divorce, says the Lord God of Israel"
2:17 'You have wearied the Lord with your words'
3:6–18 warning about stealing from God
4:2 'The sun of righteousness will rise with healing in his wings'

Further reading suggestions

John Drane, *Introducing the Old Testament*, Oxford: Lion, 1986.

W. S. Lasor, D. A. Hubbard and F. W. Bush, *Old Testament Survey*, second edition, Grand Rapids: Eerdmans, 1996.

CHAPTER 5

Overview of the New Testament

The New Testament story

Turning from the Old Testament to the New Testament is like picking up a biography after reading a history book. Instead of telling the story of a nation, the New Testament has a more restricted focus. It looks at one person's life and its impact. This said, that one person's life is viewed in the light of the Old Testament. The Old Testament has prepared the way for God's story to come to its climax. In the New Testament the promise and blessing that were originally given to Abraham appear in the form of Jesus, God's Son. The New Testament brings together different witnesses and different documents, though each is passionate about this one life and its influence. But unlike most biographies, there is no attempt within the New Testament to bring together the different witnesses so that we have a unified account. Neither are the relative strengths of each testimony evaluated: each simply stands in its own right with its own perspective. This is what makes the New Testament such a compelling read. All kinds of people in different locations wrote stories and letters, and these were in turn preserved, collected and collated into the New Testament in order to preserve the memory of Jesus.

Nazareth, the childhood home of Jesus.

The New Testament writers are not distant chroniclers looking back at someone known in the pages of history; they are instead people who often had first-hand knowledge of Jesus of Nazareth, and they joined early groups that perpetuated his name.

The New Testament writings explain how Jesus came to people's notice and how people responded to him. They consider his legacy by describing the early days of the movement to which he gave rise, the movement now called 'the Christian church'. It is people who believed that Jesus really was what he claimed to be, the Son of God and the expected messiah, who tell the stories about him. For this reason, just like the Old Testament, the New Testament is as much about faith development as it is a record of historical events.

Above: A rare ancient Roman coin, c. 27 BC, with portrait of Caesar Augustus.

Right: Detail of 19th-century stained glass window depicting the nativity of Jesus Christ, St Andrew's Cathedral, Sydney.

Before the birth of Jesus (from Old Testament times to 5/6 BC)

There is approximately a 400-year gap between the end of the Old Testament and the start of the New Testament.

During this time the Jewish people were subjected to the rule of the Persians and then the Greeks (following the campaigns of Alexander the Great in 332 BC). The Jews found themselves vulnerable as Alexander's successors, the Seleucid and Ptolemaic powers, controlled the areas around them. They generally kept a low profile but eventually rebelled against a Seleucid king (Antiochus IV Epiphanes, 175–164 BC) who wanted to impose Greek culture on them. Although the Jews survived under the leadership of Judas Maccabeus, his dynasty could do nothing when the Roman leader Pompey arrived in Jerusalem in 63 BC. Very quickly Judea became part of the Roman province called Syria. At first the Roman rulers gave the Jews certain privileges and seemed to tolerate their religious lifestyle. The Roman road system and the universality of the Greek language brought a period of unity and relative peace. However, when Jesus was born, Caesar Augustus (27 BC – AD 14) governed the Roman empire. He was responsible for consolidating the Roman empire and embarked on extensive building projects. The Jews found themselves increasingly vulnerable in Roman society and longed for a time when God would send someone to rescue them from Roman rule.

Jesus' birth and early life (from 5/6 BC to AD 7/8)

Jesus was born in a small town called Bethlehem in Judea. His parents were Mary and Joseph (see chapter 6, **Mary and Joseph**), from Nazareth in Galilee. It was an exciting time for his family. Their relatives Zechariah and Elizabeth had just seen the arrival of their first son, John (later to become known as John the Baptist) (see chapter 6, **John the Baptist**), and these two baby boys brought great joy. Both families believed that something special was going on. Mary, Joseph and Zechariah had angels visit them before their sons were born. For Zechariah and Mary this led to outbursts of prophetic praise and song. But the special things did not stop there. When

Jesus was born, something happened on the hillside to startle some shepherds: they saw angels, rushed to Bethlehem, saw the baby Jesus and started praising God too. Jesus was circumcised on the eighth day and was presented in the Temple, causing another outburst of prophecy, this time from a man called Simeon and an old prophet named Anna. A couple of years later strangers arrived at the family's home: travellers from the east had seen a special star that led them to Jesus. They brought with them rather unusual gifts.

We know little about the rest of Jesus' early years except that his parents went up to Jerusalem for the feast of the Passover every year. When Jesus was twelve years old, he went with them but his parents lost him for three days: while they travelled home, Jesus talked with teachers in the Temple courts, where again he caused something of a disturbance.

The rest of Jesus' childhood and young adult life receives no attention in the biography that the New Testament provides. It is likely that he stayed at the family home working in his father's trade as a carpenter. His birth had been remarkable, his young adult life unremarkable. The next major event was his baptism.

Jesus' ministry (from AD 27 to AD 30)

John, the son of Zechariah and Elizabeth, started to talk about repentance and baptism. He preached that someone would come who would be greater than he was, squashing the growing rumours that John himself was the expected messiah or 'Christ'.

John baptized Jesus in the River Jordan. Jesus then spent forty days alone in the wilderness before returning to Galilee to teach in the synagogues. From this point onwards, public ministry now replaced his private life. News about Jesus the teacher seemed to spread quickly and crowds would follow Jesus around. He spent much of his time around Lake Galilee and called people to be his followers, providing instruction on how they should live. Along with preaching he engaged in a healing ministry that crossed social and religious barriers and included raising the dead, healing lepers and delivering people possessed by demons. There were other kinds of miracles recorded, too, like feeding 5,000 people from a child's packed lunch. As all this was going on, people started to discuss the impact Jesus was making: was he a prophet like John or Elijah? Or maybe he was the Christ, the promised messiah whom God would send to deliver his people? Some of Jesus' closest friends said they heard a voice from heaven declaring that Jesus was the Son of God. These discussions got Jesus into trouble. The more he preached, the more he challenged the religious *status quo* and the more opposition he seemed to provoke.

Jesus started to head towards Jerusalem. He undertook both teaching and healing on the way, but the New Testament concentrates on the very last week of his life, spent in

1893 image of Jesus being baptized.

Jesus enters Jerusalem
on a donkey, from the
Church of the Ascension
Augusta Victoria,
Jerusalem.

Map of Jesus' world

0   60 km

0   40 miles

Sidon

Mt Hermon

Caesarea Philippi
(Banias)

Tyre

*Mediterranean
Sea*

Lake
Semechonitis

UPPER
GALILEE

GAULANITIS

Bethsaida-Julias

Ptolemais
(Acre)

GALILEE

Gamla

BATANEA

TRACHONITIS

Cana

*Sea of
Gennesaret*

Sepphoris

Tiberias

Nazareth

Yarmuk

AURANITIS

Gadara

DECAPOLIS

Caesarea
Maritima

Pella

Mt Carmel

Valley of Jezreel

Gilboa Mts

Gerasa
(Jerash)

Samaria
(Sebaste)

Jabbok

Plain of Sharon

Samarian Hills

Joppa
(Jaffa)

JUDEA

PERAEA

Rabbah
(Ammon)

Lydda
(Lod)

Bethel Hills

Emmaus
(Nicopolis)

Jericho
(Tel es-Sultan)

Jerusalem

Bethany

Qumran

Mt Nebo

Bethlehem

Herodium

Ashkelon

Shephelah

Judean Desert

Hebron

*Asphaltic
Sea*

Machaerus

Arnon

Besor

Masada

The Negev

Zered

Jordan

The beginnings of the Christian church (AD 30 to AD 100)

And that should have been the end of the story. We have followed the man Jesus from birth to death. His life story is complete. But Jesus' disciples claimed that they saw Jesus after his death. They believed that he came back to life and met with his friends in various situations and groups before he literally ascended into heaven before their very eyes.

Left: Depiction of the Crucifixion of Jesus Christ.

Above: This cave cut from rock near the Damascus Gate is thought by some to have been the tomb of Jesus.

The results were remarkable. The followers of Jesus experienced another supernatural event. They interpreted their experience as the fulfilment of Jesus' words that they would receive his Spirit, who would stay with them for ever. Their faith and their confidence grew. Peter began to preach to the people, as did others who had not known Jesus, such as Saul (later Paul), who left behind his Jewish fanaticism and became a 'Christian' (a follower of Christ). Others, such as Stephen who was stoned to death, suffered persecution on account of their faith but, despite all the opposition, the Christian community flourished and spread (see chapter 6, **Peter, Paul, Stephen**).

The Christian message spreads

The flourishing of the Christian community and the spreading of the Christian message

Jerusalem. It was only a week but it occupies about one third of the Gospel accounts of Jesus' life. For the Gospel writers it was in these events that Jesus' significance lay. He arrived on a donkey, to the acclaims of the crowds, but quickly found himself sharing his Last Supper with his friends as the conspiracy against him, involving even Judas his follower, started to unfold. The last night before his arrest Jesus spent alone in prayer. Then, mocked by guards and condemned to death by Pontius Pilate, the Roman prefect of Judea, he died on a cross between two thieves and was buried in a tomb cut into the rock.

Why did Jesus die?

There are two main ways we can answer this question. The first looks at the historical events surrounding Jesus' death; the second looks at the theological reasons Christians believe lie behind the death of Jesus:

1. *Historical reasons:* Jesus was seen as a troublemaker who was a threat to the Roman authorities. He was disliked (or misunderstood) by Jewish authorities, whose authority and teaching he challenged. His claim to be divine was rejected and therefore considered as blasphemy.

2. *Theological reasons:* Jesus' death was the very reason why he came to earth in the first place. God had planned to redeem the world from sin by the death of his son Jesus Christ. He was the perfect sacrifice, subject to human life but his death secured for us forgiveness and salvation.

So the New Testament claims at least three reasons for Jesus' death:
- Jesus was rejected by people
- Jesus' death was planned by God
- Jesus expected and chose the cross.

Peter's sermon to the crowd gathered on the Day of Pentecost begins by making these two points clear:

Jesus of Nazareth was a man accredited by God to you by miracles, wonders and signs, which God did among you through him, as you yourselves know. This man was handed over to you by God's set purpose and foreknowledge; and you with the help of wicked men, put him to death by nailing him to the cross. But God raised him from the dead,

freeing him form the agony of death, because it was impossible for death to keep its hold of him.

In other words, just as Jesus himself is both human and divine, so his death has divine and human elements.

Here are some of the images used in the Bible to describe the significance of Jesus' death:
- It was an example of God's love for the world (John 3:16)
- It was a sacrifice of the guiltless one on behalf of the guilty (John 1:29)
- It was a battle with the forces of evil (John 12:31)
- It was a ransom paid for humanity (Mark 10:45; 1 Corinthians 6:19–20)
- It was the way in which God's justice was satisfied and forgiveness becomes available (1 Peter 2:24; Hebrews 10:10)
- It secured the possibility of eternal life for it was followed by Jesus' own resurrection (Romans 8:33-39)
- It showed Jesus' obedience to the father (John 14:28–31)
- It was the means by which Jesus' glory was shown to the world (John 13:31–32)
- It is the way in which we can be put right with God (Romans 3:24–25)
- It is the means by which we can now have relationship with God (Hebrews 10:19–22)

It is better to think of these ideas as complementary in the sense that they add to the whole picture of why Jesus died. When we restrict our focus, and emphasise one image or idea, we lose sight of the whole.

were largely due in the early years to the journeys of Paul (formerly Saul), who decided that the good news of Jesus must be made known to Jews and Gentiles alike. This understanding that Jesus' message was relevant to all people was a recognition of the fact that Jesus' own ministry had reached out beyond the boundaries of any one national or ethnic group. So Paul went to Greece, Cyprus, Turkey, Italy and probably Spain. He supported Christian communities by his visits and by writing letters. His letters tell us about the early years of the Christian church – what it believed, issues it faced, how it organized itself. But while the church grew, tension increased, not only between Christians and the political and religious authorities but also between the Jews and the Romans. The Jews rebelled against Roman rule in AD 66, but they were not strong enough for the new Roman world power, and in AD 70 the Romans destroyed the Temple in Jerusalem.

What is clear is that the life of Jesus had changed the known world. The story

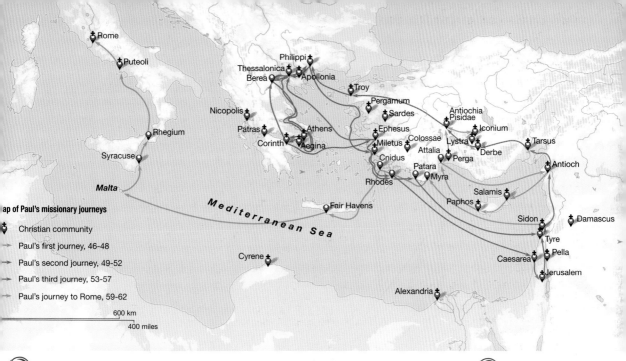

Map of Paul's missionary journeys

- ⛪ Christian community
- → Paul's first journey, 46–48
- → Paul's second journey, 49–52
- → Paul's third journey, 53–57
- → Paul's journey to Rome, 59–62

600 km
400 miles

The New Testament writers and the use of the Old Testament

The New Testament writers draw on the Old Testament as they write about Jesus and try to explain his significance. Sometimes they simply allude to Old Testament verses and ideas. At other times they quote directly from the Old Testament. The epistle to the Hebrews has many Old Testament quotations, as do the Gospels – take a look at Matthew's Gospel particularly. Quotation from the Old Testament also occurs in the sermons in Acts and in the theological discussions in Paul's and Peter's letters (see, for example, Romans 9–11; 1 Peter 1–5).

that began in New Testament times goes on today. It's the story of a faith focused around one man who lived for about thirty years in one part of the world. But his contemporaries, like many Christians today, could not keep the faith they had discovered in Jesus to themselves. (See chapter 5, **Overview of the New Testament**; chapter 6, **The family of Jesus**.)

An explanation of terms:

Gospel means 'good news' and was associated with the good news of the birth of a political deliverer or a saviour of the people.

89

New Testament events

400–5/6 BC

◆ 5/6 BC The birth of Jesus

5/6 BC – AD 7/8

Jesus' early life:

◆ Jesus circumcised eight days after birth
◆ Magi arrive to visit Jesus (approx. two years later)
◆ Jesus visits the Temple (aged twelve)

◆ Jesus brought up in family home

Events in the Roman world

400–5/6 BC

◆ 332 BC Campaigns of Alexander the Great
◆ 175–163 BC Antiochus IV Epiphanes
◆ 168 BC Maccabean Revolt
◆ 63 BC Pompey arrives in Jerusalem and Roman domination of Judea begins (lasts to AD 330)
◆ 43 BC Julius Caesar assassinated
◆ 37–4 BC Herod the Great rules Judea
◆ 27 BC – AD 14 Emperor Caesar Augustus

5/6 BC – AD 7/8

◆ AD 14–37 Emperor Tiberius

New Testament events	Events in the Roman world
AD 27–30	**AD 27–30**
Jesus' public ministry:	◆ AD 26–36 Pilate is Roman governor in Judea
◆ Jesus is baptized ◆ Jesus' ministry in Galilee ◆ Jesus' ministry in Jerusalem ◆ Jesus' trial ◆ Jesus' death and resurrection	
AD 30–100	**AD 30–100**
Beginnings of the Christian church:	◆ AD 37–41 Emperor Gaius Caligula
◆ The day of Pentecost ◆ Peter's ministry ◆ Stephen is martyred (c. AD 31/32) ◆ Saul's conversion (c. AD 33) ◆ Paul's journeys to Greece, Cyprus, Turkey and Spain (AD 46–58) ◆ Jerusalem Council (AD 48)	◆ AD 41–54 Emperor Claudius ◆ Jews expelled from Rome (AD 49)
◆ Letters written to newly founded Christian churches and individuals	
◆ Peter and Paul die (c. AD 65)	◆ AD 54–68 Emperor Nero ◆ Fire in Rome (AD 64) ◆ AD 69–79 Emperor Vespasian
◆ New Testament Gospels are compiled	
◆ Paul imprisoned in Rome	◆ AD 70 Romans destroy the Temple in Jerusalem ◆ AD 79–81 Emperor Titus ◆ AD 81–96 Emperor Domitian ◆ AD 96–98 Emperor Nerva
◆ John imprisoned on Patmos	◆ AD 98–117 Emperor Trajan
◆ Late letters and Revelation written	

The order of books in the New Testament

The present order of the literature in the New Testament does not reflect the order in which these texts were written. For example, the Gospels come first, but although they present accounts of the events in Jesus' lifetime they were composed after the early New Testament letters, which are concerned with the church as it developed after Jesus' life. It is impossible to be very precise about the dating of every New Testament text, but the following table gives a basic outline of the writing order of the New Testament.

c. AD 50–65	Galatians
	James?
	1 Thessalonians
	Philippians
	Philemon
	1 Corinthians
	Romans
	2 Corinthians
	2 Thessalonians?

c. AD 65–100	Colossians?
	Ephesians?
	Mark's Gospel
	Hebrews?
	Luke's Gospel
	Matthew's Gospel
	John's Gospel
	Acts
	Revelation
	1, 2 and 3 John
	1 Peter
	1 and 2 Timothy
	Titus
	2 Peter
	Jude?

The New Testament books

Matthew's Gospel

'This took place to fulfil what was spoken through the prophet...'

Theme: Matthew's Gospel (probably compiled between AD 75 and 85) draws on Mark (the earliest Gospel to be written) and on other sources to tell us about Jesus. Matthew presents Jesus as the one who fulfils Old Testament prophecy, the Jews' long-awaited messiah. Jesus' most famous teaching, the Sermon on the Mount, uses Old Testament terminology and ideas, and shows that Jesus is the new Moses who teaches a new Law. He is also the guarantor of God's presence among God's people. God has given him authority: he brings God's kingdom on earth and his message is for all people. For Matthew, becoming a follower of Jesus (discipleship) means obeying him.

Main characters: Jesus, John the Baptist and the disciples.

Well-known passages:
5–7 the Sermon on the Mount;
6:9–15 the Lord's Prayer
16 Peter says Jesus is the messiah
20 the parable of the vineyard workers
25 parables of the ten virgins and talents
28 the Great Commission

Structure:
1–2 prologue
3–28 narratives leading up to five main teaching sections:
5–7, 10, 13, 18, 24–25
28:16–20 epilogue

An aerial view of the so-called Mount of the Beatitudes, where Jesus is said to have preached the Sermon on the Mount. A church occupies the top of the hill, overlooking the north end of the Sea of Galilee, near Tabgha.

Right: Detail of the *Passion of Jesus Christ*, from the Sacred Heart Church, Sydney, Australia.

Mark's Gospel

'If anyone would come after me he must deny himself and take up his cross and follow me.'

Theme: Mark's was probably the earliest Gospel to be written, between AD 66 and 70.

Well-known passages:
13 Jesus' teaching about the end times
16:1–8 a short resurrection story

Structure:
1–9 Jesus' public ministry around Lake Galilee
10 Jesus teaches his disciples in Judea
11–16 Jesus' final week in Jerusalem

Mark stresses Jesus' authority as teacher, healer, the Lord of the sabbath and the one able to forgive sins. Sometimes Mark's Gospel portrays Jesus as trying to keep his messianic identity secret. The Gospel contains less of Jesus' teaching than the other Gospels, concentrating instead on the action. It gives particular attention to Jesus' final week, and the climax is reached at the moment of Jesus' death when the centurion declares, 'Surely this man was the Son of God' (15:39). At this moment of apparent weakness, Jesus' divinity comes to the fore. Mark tells Jesus' disciples to expect suffering but to know that Jesus has walked that path before them.

Main characters: Jesus and his disciples.

Luke's Gospel

'The Spirit of the Lord is upon me... to proclaim good news to the poor.'

Theme: written probably between AD 60 and 80, Luke's Gospel is the first part of an orderly account that the writer initially produced for the benefit of someone called Theophilus, who may have been a Roman official. Its theme is the joy of salvation. The good news of Jesus is for everyone, so Jesus shows a special interest in vulnerable people, especially poor people and women, as well as religious and social misfits (such as Samaritans and tax collectors). Jesus' prayers punctuate the Gospel: he prays before every main event in his life. Nearly half the material in Luke is unique, but the events of Jesus' last week are consistent with Mark and Matthew. Luke's account stands out because of the compassionate words of Jesus during his last week and on the cross, dominated by concern for his disciples and those around him.

Well-known passages:
4 Jesus reads from Isaiah at Nazareth
10 parable of the good Samaritan
15 parable of the prodigal son
19 Jesus meets Zacchaeus
24 the risen Jesus meets two people on the Emmaus road

Structure:
1–2 Jesus' birth and early life
3–9 Jesus in Galilee
10–19 Jesus in Judea
20–24 Jesus' final week in Jerusalem

Main characters: Jesus, his disciples, the poor and the outcasts of society.

John's Gospel

'For God so loved the world that he gave his one and only Son that whoever believes on him should not perish but have eternal life.'

Well-known passages:
1 the prologue: 'In the beginning was the Word'
2 Jesus changes water into wine
3 Jesus tells Nicodemus he must be born again
9 Jesus heals a blind man
11 Jesus raises Lazarus from the dead
13 Jesus washes his disciples' feet
14–16 Jesus teaches his disciples for the last time; including about the Holy Spirit
17 Jesus prays
21 the risen Jesus talks with Simon Peter

Structure:
1 prologue
2–17 signs followed by discourses
18–19 Jesus' final week and his death
20–21 resurrection encounters with Christ

(See also chapter 9, **Who is Jesus? What is Jesus Like?**)

Theme: John's Gospel is quite distinct from the other Gospels, and was probably written after them. The author describes himself as 'the disciple whom Jesus loved'. Some people suggest that this John is unlikely to be John the apostle, not least because he would have been in extreme old age at the probable time of writing. It begins with an outstanding prologue (John 1:1–18) that incorporates Greek concepts about God's word (Greek *logos*) and the wisdom behind the universe. It concentrates on Jesus' identity and contains some unique statements of Jesus about his own nature and ministry. The 'I am' sayings are among the most well-known claims about himself that Jesus made. This Gospel was written so that its readers might 'believe that Jesus is the Christ' (20:31). Jesus is described as both truly human (with human emotions and feelings) and truly divine. His relationship to the Father and to the Holy Spirit is also explored. Jesus' death is portrayed as his glory and the second half of the Gospel takes this as its primary theme.

Main characters: Jesus and his disciples (especially Peter and John).

The Raising of Lazarus (1886–94), by James Tissot.

Right: Image of a gold plated mosaic depicting the apostle Paul in the Hagia Sofia, Istanbul, Turkey.

Acts of the Apostles

'The Lord added to their number daily those who were being saved.'

Well-known passages:
1 Jesus ascends into heaven
2 the day of Pentecost when the Spirit comes
2:42–47 description of early church life
7 the death of Stephen
8 Philip and the Ethiopian eunuch
9 Saul's conversion on the road to Damascus
10 Peter's vision
12 Peter escapes from prison
16 Lydia is converted and baptized
27 Paul is shipwrecked

Structure:
1–7 the church in Jerusalem: in the power of the Spirit
8–15 the church expands: the Spirit and the acts of Peter
16–20 the Spirit and the acts of Paul: missionary journeys
21–28 Paul's sufferings

Theme: continuing the story of his Gospel, Luke gives an account of the spread of the Christian message in Jerusalem and then further afield by focusing on two apostles: Peter and Paul. Luke's concern is not to follow their every move but to show that the good news about Jesus continued to be announced by Christians through the power of the Holy Spirit. Luke gives examples of Christian preaching and faith to show Theophilus – and all of us – that Jesus is reigning in heaven and that God's eternal purposes, which began with Israel, are being fulfilled. He especially emphasizes the unity of the church, in prayer and praise and through the commitment of its members to each other. He deals with a thirty-year period of church history ending in about AD 60.

Main characters: Stephen, Philip, Peter, Paul, Barnabas and Timothy.

Romans

'I am not ashamed of the gospel because it is the power of God for the salvation of everyone.'

Well-known passages:
4 the faith of Abraham
8 'The Spirit of God lives in you'
8:28–39 'Nothing can separate us from the love of God in Christ'
12 'Offer your bodies as living sacrifices'

Structure:
1–2 all people need saving from sin
3–11 all people are saved from sin through faith in Christ
12–15 all people who are saved through Christ will live accordingly
16 Paul's farewell greetings

Theme: Romans is a letter addressed to Christians who were probably meeting in scattered homes throughout the

large city of Rome. They were experiencing some teething problems in setting up agreed standards of practice and living. Paul wrote to help them, but his priority was to show them what the gospel is – how people can be put into a right relationship with God – and how the gospel's message needs to be shared and celebrated. In this they would find their unity. This is the most systematic of Paul's letters and contains some weighty theological sections.

1 Corinthians

'To... those sanctified in Christ Jesus and called to be his holy people.'

Well-known passages:
1 Christ is the wisdom of God
7 instructions about marriage
11 instructions about worship and the Lord's Supper
12 the church is the body of Christ
13 'Love is...'
15 teaching about the resurrection

Structure:
1–10 principles for Christian living
11–14 principles for Christian worship
15 teaching about resurrection
16 Paul's farewell greetings

Theme: this is the first of two New Testament letters that Paul wrote to the Christians at Corinth – he probably wrote other letters to the church there too, because there was a lot to sort out. Part of the reason for this was the nature of the city itself. It was known as a centre for prostitution, not least connected to its many pagan temples. It was also a busy commercial centre with two ports and many resulting and pervasive influences. Paul writes this letter to put the church right in regards to its character (there were divisions and disputes), practice (the Lord's Supper [see glossary], worship gatherings) and teaching (especially about the resurrection of Jesus and of believers).

2 Corinthians

'For it is not the one who commends himself who is approved, but the one whom the Lord commends.'

Theme: in this more personal letter to Corinth Paul defends his own ministry and authority. He demonstrates his care for the Corinthian Christians and longs to visit them again. He asks them to be loyal to him. It is possible that this is actually a collection of letters to the church at Corinth which have come together as they were circulated.

Well-known passages:
4 God's all-surpassing power
11 Paul boasts in his sufferings
12:8 'My grace is sufficient for you...'

Structure:
1–7 Paul defends his apostolic ministry
8–9 the matter of monetary collections
10–13 Paul defends his authority

Left: Corinth was a major port in ancient Greece that was famous for its wealth, athletics, but also its pagan temples and immorality.

Galatians

'So the law was put in charge to lead us to Christ so that we might be justified by faith.'

Theme: with a growing number of Gentile converts among the Christian community in the region of Galatia, Paul writes to emphasize to the Jewish church members that to insist that Gentiles adhere to Old Testament ceremonial law (especially circumcision) is pointless. With vigour and determination, Paul stresses that salvation comes by faith in Jesus and by that faith alone. He urges the church to live in a way that reflects the truth of their freedom in Christ.

Well-known passages:
2:20 'I have been crucified with Christ…'
3:26 – 4:7 'There is neither Jew nor Greek, slave nor free, male nor female…'
5:22–23 'The fruit of the Spirit is…'

Structure:
1–4 have faith in Christ alone
5–6 live in the freedom of Christ

Ephesians

Theme: Paul writes to Christians at Ephesus reminding them of the essential truths of the Christian faith. He tells them who Christ is, who they are in Christ and how they should respond by living 'a life of love, just as Christ loved us'. Faith in Christ results in lives of peace in the church, in society and in family life.

Well-known passages:
1 hymn of praise to 'the God and Father of our Lord Jesus Christ'
3 Paul's prayer for the Ephesian Christians
5:22–6:4 family relationships: wives and husbands, parents and children
6:10–17 putting on the armour of God

Structure:
1–3 the privileges of being 'in Christ'
4–6 the responsibilities of being 'in Christ'

Ephesus was the most important Greek city in Ionian Asia Minor. The amphitheatre, which held approximately 25,000 spectators, was was first constructed in the 3rd century BC, then renovated under first emperor Claudius then Emperor Trajan in the 1st century AD. It is still used as a performance space today.

Philippians

Theme: Paul writes this letter to thank the church for a gift, to encourage them, to warn them about false teachers, to send his greetings and to commend Timothy and Epaphroditus to them. On the whole, the letter is a joyful one, which is surprising in the light of the fact that Paul wrote it from prison. Paul rejoices in the friendships at Philippi and the goodness of God.

Well-known passages:
1:21 for me, to live is Christ
2 the hymn in praise of Jesus
2:15 'shine like stars'
3:14 'I press on towards the goal to win the prize for which God has called me'
4:13 'I can do everything through him who gives me strength'

Structure:
1 Paul is thankful for the church
2–4 Paul appeals to the church to be joyful and Christlike

Colossians

Theme: written from prison to a group of people that, as far as we know, Paul never met, Colossians takes care at the start and the end to ensure that it is well received. Paul offers prayers for these Christians and he warns, instructs, and commends them.

Well-known passages:
1 the supremacy of Jesus Christ
3:1 'Set your hearts on things above'

Structure:
1 introduction
2–4 guidelines for holy living

1 Thessalonians

Theme: possibly written after 2 Thessalonians, this letter suggests that there were ongoing problems in a church where young Christians, mainly Jewish, misunderstood some basic Christian teaching. Paul describes Jesus as the king who has come and is to come and uses Jewish apocalyptic language that would have been familiar to his readers. Paul wants to encourage the Christians to remain strong in their faith and practice.

Well-known passages:
3:11–13 Paul's prayer for the church
4:13 – 5:11 teaching about Christ's second coming

Structure:
1–3 Paul encourages the persecuted Christians
4–5 Paul instructs them in Christian faith and practice

2 Thessalonians

'May our Lord Jesus Christ himself, and God the Father who loved us and by his grace gave us eternal encouragement and hope, encourage your hearts and strengthen you in every good deed and word.'

Well-known passage:
2 the man of lawlessness

Structure:
1 Paul praises the church
2 Paul instructs the church
3 Paul asks for prayer

Theme: Paul writes this brief letter to address three issues. First, the practical problem that a small young church was suffering threats; secondly, confusion about the idea of a day of the Lord; thirdly, the need for Christians to work hard for their living. For this frail church, Paul fills his letter with prayers and encouragement.

1 Timothy

Theme: 1 Timothy, 2 Timothy and Titus are sometimes referred to as 'pastoral letters'. They possibly originate with Paul, or with one of his followers. Contained in 1 Timothy are instructions about how to look after the church at Ephesus. The letter deals with issues relating to doctrine (challenging those who promoted Jewish strictures), church practice (worship, church leaders, how Timothy should exercise oversight), the nature of a preaching ministry, and Christian living (caring for the needy).

Well-known passages:
2:9–15 women in the church
3:16 the mystery of godliness
4:12 don't let anyone look down on you because you are young

Structure:
1 warning against false teaching
2–3 instructions about Christian worship and leadership
4–5 instructions to Timothy about his role

Timothy with his mother (Eunice) and grandmother (Lois) are depicted in this stained glass from St Mildred's Church, Tenterden, Kent. Paul commends all three for their faith (2 Timothy 1:5).

2 Timothy

Theme: sometimes understood as presenting the summary of Paul's faith and teaching, this letter was probably written at the end of his life while he endured harsh conditions in prison under Nero. The writer anticipates that he will pay the ultimate price for his faith and encourages those who might face similar trials.

Well-known passages:
3:16–17 the inspiration of Scripture
4:6–8 Paul predicts his own death: 'I have fought the good fight, I have finished the race...'

Structure:
1–2 Paul encourages Timothy
3–4 Paul instructs Timothy

Titus

Theme: again attributed to Paul, this letter is addressed to Titus, whom Paul had left in Crete to set up the church there. Titus is given guidance on practical issues, including appointing elders, dealing with opposition and deciding what to teach. He is instructed about the importance of good living, including conduct in Christian households. But such teaching begins with confidence in the gospel itself, which is summarized twice (2:11–14 and 3:3–7).

Well-known passages:
2:11–14; 3:3–7 summaries of the gospel message

Structure:
1 Paul clarifies Titus's task
2–3 Paul gives instructions for the church community

Philemon

Theme: Paul writes a persuasive letter to a Christian at Colossae asking him to welcome back a runaway slave, Onesimus, as a Christian brother.

Structure:
greetings, thanksgiving, pleas, farewell greetings

Bust of the emperor Nero (c. 54–68 AD), an early persecutor of Christians.

Hebrews

'Since we have a great high priest who has gone through the heavens, Jesus the Son of God, let us hold firmly to the faith we profess.'

Theme: although this New Testament book does have farewell greetings, it doesn't have any opening greetings. In character and content it reads more like a sermon than a letter. The main subject is the person and work of Jesus Christ. He is supreme and, above all, the one who fulfils the Old Testament, the high priest and the once-for-all sacrifice for sins. Highly reliant on a good grasp of the Old Testament, it was written to Jewish Christians (hence its title), most likely by someone other than Paul, probably before AD 70.

Well-known passages:
4:14 – 5:8 Jesus as the great high priest
7 Jesus compared to Melchizedek
11 the Old Testament gallery of faith
12 'Let us fix our eyes on Jesus'

Structure:
1–3 Jesus is supreme over all
4–10 Jesus is the supreme high priest
11–13 Christians must be thankful, faithful worshippers of God

James

'Faith without deeds is useless.'

Theme: this is sometimes considered the earliest piece of writing preserved in the New Testament, originating with James (the brother of Jesus). The 'letter' does not have the normal farewell greetings and, like Hebrews, can be read as a sermon. It has Jewish overtones, even locating the Christians as gathering in synagogues (2:2). It adopts ideas common in wisdom literature (see chapter 3), taking the nature of true faith as its dominant theme.

Well-known passages:
3 taming the tongue
4:7–10 'Submit yourself, then, to God'
5:13–18 praying for healing

Structure:
1 faith in trials
2–4 faith in practice
5 faith in suffering

Statues of Old Testament figures Melchizedek, Abraham preparing to sacrifice Isaac, and Moses from the north portal of Chartres Cathedral, France.

1 Peter

Theme: 1 Peter is a letter offering practical advice and encouragement to a church often misunderstood by those around and facing imminent persecution. It was probably written in Nero's reign, so Peter's own martyrdom was relatively imminent. Its purpose was to encourage and to offer hope. It contains many exhortations that give the letter a sermonic feel. This along with the baptismal theme has led to the suggestion that the content is mainly a baptismal sermon.

Well-known passages:
2:4–8 Christ the living stone
2:9 'You are a chosen people, a holy nation, a people belonging to God...'
4:8 'Love covers a multitude of sins'
5:7 'Cast all your anxiety on him because he cares for you'

Structure:
1 – 2:12 Christians have a living hope based in Christ
2:13–15 Christians must live in the light of their hope

2 Peter

'Be on your guard so you may not be carried away by the error of lawless men and fall from your secure position.'

Theme: 2 Peter is a letter concerning trouble from within the church caused by false teachers who create doubts by slandering God and his purposes. Christians are encouraged to make their 'calling and election sure'. They are reminded that the day of God's justice and glory will come.

Well-known passages:
3:9: 'The Lord is not slow in keeping his promise... he is patient with you'
3:10 'The day of the Lord will come like a thief'

Structure:
1 Christian hope
2 the judgment that false teachers face
3 the coming day of the Lord

1 John

Theme: without the normal greetings, or even a stated author, this letter launches straight into its theme: fellowship with the Father through Jesus. The writer speaks of God's great love and how love should mark our relationships with others.

Well-known passages (1 John):
1:9 'If we confess our sins...'
3:1 'How great is the love the Father has lavished on us'
4:7 'Dear friends, let us love one another, for love comes from God'
4:8, 16 'God is love'
4:19 'We love because he first loved us'

Structure (1 John):
1 the gospel of Jesus
2–4 living in the light of God's love
5 faith in Jesus

Structure (2 John):
Greeting; warning about deceivers; farewell greetings

Structure (3 John):
Greetings; response to other Christians; farewell greetings

2 John

Theme: 2 John is a short note to a church or an individual encouraging a lifestyle of love that is nonetheless wary of deceivers.

3 John

Theme: in writing this personal note to his friend Gaius, John mentions two men. He is concerned about Diotrephes but commends Demetrius.

Detail of John the Evangelist, from the altarpiece of St Mark's Cathedral, Venice, c.1488–90, by Sandro Botticelli.

Jude
'To him who is able to keep you from falling...'

Theme: Jude writes to warn 'those who are loved by God' about godless, immoral people. Christian people can take encouragement from the fact that God is able to preserve and keep them.

Well-known passage:
24–25 the doxology

Structure:
Greeting; warning against godless people; encouragement to stay faithful to God

Revelation

'Behold I am coming soon... I am the Alpha and the Omega, the First and the Last, the Beginning and the End.'

Well-known passages:
1:12–16 the vision of Jesus
2:4 'You have forsaken your first love'
3:15 'You are neither hot nor cold'
3:20 'Here I am. I stand at the door and knock'
5:9 'You are worthy to take the scroll and open the seals'
7 the lamb and the 144,000
18 woes to Babylon
19 hallelujahs ring from heaven
21 vision of the New Jerusalem
22 'I am coming soon'

Structure:
1 introduction
2–3 letters to seven churches
4–5 vision of heaven
6–20 a series of apocalyptic visions
21 the Christian hope: a new heaven and earth; the New Jerusalem; the coming of Jesus

Theme: alternatively called 'the Apocalypse of John' (see chapter 3, **Apocalyptic literature**) Revelation is written in the style of a letter, contains many visions and is full of imagery. It was probably composed in the reign of Domitian, in the last decade of the first century, when Christians faced persecution. The writer reassures Christians that God reigns in heaven and that all God's purposes in history will be fulfilled when Jesus' glory is revealed. In other words, the present difficulties the Christians face are not the whole reality: the victory of God is certain.

Parables and Miracles

The gospels concentrate on the teaching and miracles of Jesus. The following tables provide details of where these are recorded in the Gospel accounts.

Map showing the seven churches of Asia Minor (Revelation 2–3).

Parables of Jesus	Matthew	Mark	Luke	John
lamp under a bowl	5:14–16	4:21–22	8:16; 11:33	
houses on rock and on sand	7:24–27		6:47–49	
new cloth on an old garment	9:16	2:21	5:36	
new wine in old wineskins	9:17	2:22	5:37–39	
sower and soils	13:3–8	4:3–8	8:5–8	
mustard seed	13:31–32	4:30–32	13:18–19	
weeds	13:24–30			
yeast	13:33		13:20–21	
hidden treasure	13:44			
pearl of great value	13:45–46			
net	13:47–50			
lost sheep	18:12–14		15:4–7	
two debtors (unforgiving servant)	18:23–35			
workers in the vineyard	20:1–16			
two sons	21:28–31			
wicked tenants	21:33–43	12:1–9	20:9–16	
invitation to the wedding feast; man without a wedding garment	22:2–14			
fig tree as herald of summer	24:32–33	13:28–29	21:29–31	
ten 'bridesmaids'	25:1–13			
talents (Matthew); pounds (Luke)	25:14–30		19:12–27	
sheep and goats	25:31–46			
seedtime to harvest		4:26–29		
creditor and the debtors			7:41–43	
good Samaritan			10:30–37	
friend in need			11:5–10	
rich fool			12:16–21	
alert servants			12:35–40	
faithful steward			12:42–48	

Parables of Jesus cont'd	Matthew	Mark	Luke	John
fig-tree without figs			13:6–9	
places of honour at the wedding feast			14:7–14	
great banquet and the reluctant guests			14:16–24	
counting the cost			14:28–33	
lost coin			15:8–10	
the lost son			15:11–32	
shrewd manager			16:1–8	
rich man and Lazarus			16:19–31	
the master and his servant			17:7–10	
the persistent widow and the unrighteous judge			18:2–8	
the Pharisee and the tax-collector			18:10–14	

Miracles of Jesus	Matthew	Mark	Luke	John
Healing of physical and mental disorders				
leper	8:2–4	1:40–42	5:12–14	
centurion's servant	8:5–13		7:1–10	
Peter's mother-in-law	8:14–15	1:30–31	4:38–39	
many demon-possessed	8:16–17	1:32–34	4:40–41	
two Gadarenes	8:28–34	5:1–20	8:27–39	
paralysed man	9:2–8	2:3–12	5:18–25	
woman with a haemorrhage	9:20–22	5:25–34	8:43–48	
two blind men	9:27–31			
man mute and possessed	9:32–33			
man with a withered hand	12:10–13	3:1–5	6:6–10	
man blind, mute and possessed	12:22		11:14	
Canaanite woman's daughter	15:21–28	7:25–30		
boy with epilepsy	17:14–18	9:17–29	9:38–43	

Miracles of Jesus cont'd	Matthew	Mark	Luke	John
Healing of physical and mental disorders				
Bartimaeus and another blind man	20:29–34	10:46–52	18:35–43	
man possessed at the synagogue		1:23–26	4:33–35	
deaf and mute man	15:29–31	7:32–37		
blind man at Bethsaida		8:22–26		
woman bent double			13:11–13	
man with dropsy			14:1–4	
ten lepers			17:11–19	
Malchus's ear			22:50–51	
official's son at Capernaum				4:46–54
sick man, pool of Bethesda				5:2–9
man born blind				9:1–41
Command over the forces of nature				
calming of the storm	8:23–27	4:37–41	8:22–25	
walking on the water	14:25–27	6:48–51		6:19–21
5,000 people fed	14:15–21	6:35–44	9:12–17	6:5–13
4,000 people fed	15:32–38	8:1–9		
coin in the fish's mouth	17:24–27			
fig-tree withered	21:18–22	11:12–14, 20–23		
catch of fish			5:1–11	
water turned into wine				2:1–11
another catch of fish				21:4–11
Bringing the dead back to life				
Jairus's daughter	9:18–19, 23–26	5:22–24, 35–43	8:41–42, 49–56	
widow's son			7:11–15	
Lazarus				11:1–44

Individuals in the Bible

Beginnings

Adam and Eve

Adam and Eve were the first man and woman, 'made in God's image'. Eve was made from one of Adam's ribs and her role was to be Adam's helper. Far from indicating her subordination to Adam, this meant that Eve had the ability and desire to assist Adam, and, moreover, that he needed her assistance. They were told by God to be fruitful, and to rule over the earth. Together they were 'one flesh' and had equal status before God and creation. When they were tempted to disobey God, Adam and Eve both succumbed and came under God's judgment. The Adam and Eve story illustrates the consequences of sin and sets the tone for the rest of the Bible. In the New Testament Adam's name becomes representative of the human race in rebellion against God, but Adam is also seen as the first human son of God. (Genesis 1–5; Luke 3:38; Romans 5; 1 Corinthians 15.)

Cain and Abel

Cain, the firstborn son of Adam and Eve, grew crops, whereas his brother Abel tended sheep. They came into conflict when Abel's offering to the Lord proved more acceptable than that of Cain. The resulting jealousy and anger led Cain to murder Abel. He received God's curse: the land would not produce crops for him and he would become a restless wanderer.

God nevertheless protected Cain by marking him out so that no one would kill him.(Genesis 4–5; Hebrews 11; 1 John 3.)

Noah

Noah is described as a righteous, blameless man who walked with God. Noah obeyed God and built an ark to save both his family and every known breed of animal when

Cain and Abel are depicted in this window in All Saints Church, Middleton Cheney, Northamptonshire, UK.

the earth was completely flooded for 150 days. God made a covenant with Noah and promised not to flood the earth again. God set the rainbow in the sky as a sign of this promise. (Genesis 6–10; Hebrews 11; Matthew 24:36ff.).

The Patriarchs

Abraham

Abram (whose name was later changed to Abraham by God) was a shepherd. He received a call from God, who promised to bless him and make his name great. Abraham's descendants were chosen to receive the Promised Land of Canaan and to be a blessing to other nations. This established an agenda for God's people that can be traced through the rest of the Bible. He left Haran and set out for Canaan. Abraham was called the father of many, the father of the faithful and the friend of God. His wife, Sarah, was barren when Abraham received God's promise. Sarah's slave Hagar provided Abraham with a son (Ishmael), but the promise to Abraham found complete fulfilment when Sarah gave birth to Isaac. God is known elsewhere in the Bible as 'the God of Abraham', and Jesus is presented as Abraham's royal descendant (through the line of David). (Genesis 12–25; Psalm 105:5–6; Isaiah 41; Matthew 1:1; Galatians 3–4; John 8:39; Romans 4; Hebrews 11; James 2).

Isaac

Isaac was born to Abraham and Sarah in their old age, and his name means 'laughter'. This was apt because Sarah laughed in disbelief when she heard that God had promised her a son. Information about Isaac's life is sketchy, but he married Rebekah, who gave birth to twin boys, Jacob and Esau. When Isaac was still a boy, Abraham was tested by God and was prepared (though not required) to offer his son as a human sacrifice. Jacob duped Isaac in his old age in order to secure the blessing reserved for his first-born son, Esau (Genesis 21–28; Romans 9; Hebrews 11; James 2).

Jacob

Jacob was the younger of the twins born to Isaac and Rebekah. Jacob's relationship with his brother was strained from the start (they fought in the womb) and this led to Jacob's successful attempt to trick Esau and his father so as to receive the blessing and rights normally preserved for the eldest son. Jacob agreed to work for his uncle Laban for seven years in return for marriage to his cousin Rachel, but was himself tricked into marrying Rachel's older sister Leah. He then worked for another seven years in order to marry Rachel as well. He had sons with Leah and Rachel, and also with Bilhah (Rachel's maid) and Zilpah (Leah's maid), but it was Rachel's sons, Joseph and Benjamin, who were Jacob's favourites. His twelve sons headed the twelve tribes of Israel. Jacob had visions of God at Bethel and later at Peniel, where he was given the name 'Israel'. (Genesis 25–35, 46–50; Acts 7; Romans 9:10–13; Hebrews 11).

Joseph

Joseph was the firstborn son of Jacob and Rachel. Joseph's elder brothers resented Jacob's favouritism towards him (especially the gift of a many-coloured coat) and also Joseph's dreams about his own superiority over them. Eventually they sold him as a slave and he was taken to Egypt. Joseph at first received favour in the house of his Egyptian master, Potiphar, until Potiphar's wife falsely accused him of trying to seduce her. Joseph was imprisoned, but his ability to interpret dreams became widely known. After interpreting Pharaoh's dreams he was appointed Pharaoh's second-in-command, in charge of food storage and distribution during a period of famine. Joseph's brothers and father came to Egypt looking for food and, after an emotional reunion, they were reconciled with Joseph. Shortly afterwards Jacob died, and Joseph took him to Canaan to be buried. (Genesis 37–50; Acts 7; Hebrews 11).

The leaders and judges

Moses

Moses was born in Egypt to Hebrew parents. By this time the Egyptians had enslaved the Israelites and were murdering their boy children, so the infant Moses was hidden in a basket among bulrushes. Pharaoh's daughter discovered him, however, and he was brought up in Pharaoh's household. He had to flee when

Abraham leaves Haran upon receiving the call of God (Genesis 12), by Jozsef Molnar, 19th century.

he killed an Egyptian; and he married a girl from Midian, Zipporah, with whom he had two sons. His dramatic encounter with God, speaking out of a burning bush, brought a new revelation about the name and purposes of the God of Abraham. This encounter determined the mission of Moses' life – bringing the Israelites out of slavery in Egypt. With the help of his brother Aaron, and after divine intervention in the form of plagues sent against Pharaoh and Egypt, Moses led the Israelites into the Sinai wilderness where God made a covenant with them. Moses received the Ten Commandments from God and guided the Israelites in their cultural and religious life. He took them to the borders of the Promised Land, although he did not enter it himself. In the New Testament Moses is remembered as a lawgiver and the writer of the Pentateuch (Exodus; Leviticus; Numbers; Deuteronomy; Matthew 17; Luke 24; Hebrews 11).

Joshua

Joshua was a follower of Moses who became Moses' successor and led the people of Israel across the Jordan to take possession of the Promised Land. Joshua was a military leader, planning Israelite campaigns against the inhabitants of the Promised Land. He renewed the people's spiritual life, organized the division of the land and appointed Levitical priests. He is described as the servant of the Lord. 'Joshua' is equivalent to the Greek name 'Jesus'(Exodus 17; Numbers 14; Joshua; Judges 1–2; Acts 7:45).

Deborah

Deborah was one of the leaders ('judges') appointed by God to deliver the people after Joshua's death. At this time, a king in Canaan called Jabin oppressed God's people, and they asked God for help. Deborah, also a prophet, settled disputes for the people and gave advice to Barak, their military leader. She told him to attack Jabin's army and, with her help, Barak secured victory for the Israelites (Judges 4–5).

Gideon

Gideon was a judge whom God raised up when the Israelites were oppressed by the Midianites and Amalekites (see chapter 7). The angel of the Lord called Gideon a 'mighty warrior', and God instructed him

to destroy altars to pagan idols and defeat Israel's enemies. Gideon twice tested God's commitment to delivering the Israelites, demanding and receiving a miraculous sign to confirm God's promise. Following God's orders he took only 300 men to attack the Midianite army (Judges 6–8; Hebrews 11:32).

Samson

Samson was born to a woman who had been barren until an angel of the Lord told her she was to give birth to a Nazarite, a man set apart to serve God. The Spirit of the Lord worked in Samson's life, giving him amazing strength (he tore a lion apart and killed thirty men single-handedly). The Spirit also directed him to marry a Philistine. When this Philistine wife was taken from him by her father, Samson killed a thousand Philistines with an ox's jawbone. He later fell in love with and married another Philistine woman, Delilah, who persuaded him to reveal that the secret of his strength lay in his hair. Delilah cut his hair and allowed the Philistines to capture him. Facing his death Samson prayed to God for one final moment of strength and pushed down the columns supporting the temple of the god Dagon, killing himself and all the Philistines inside (Judges 13–16).

Eli

Eli was the elderly priest at a temple where the prophet Samuel's parents went to worship the Lord. Samuel became Eli's assistant, and Eli helped him to recognize God's voice. Samuel revealed to Eli that his own sons Hophni and Phinehas had brought God's judgment on his family by their wicked deeds (1 Samuel 1–4).

Samuel

Born to parents (Elkanah and Hannah) who had prayed for many years for a son, Samuel was dedicated to the Lord's service and assisted Eli as a young child. He was still a child when he heard God's voice and delivered his first words of prophecy, against the wicked sons of Eli. He was the last of the judges of Israel, organizing campaigns against the Philistines and leading the people in acts of devotion to God. Samuel anointed Israel's first two kings, Saul and David. His lifetime marked the transition from the rule of the judges to the era of monarchy (1 Samuel 1–19, 28; Acts 13:20; Hebrews 11:32).

Far left: Deborah the prophetess sings her song of praise and triumph (Judges 5) in this engraving after Gustave Doré (1833–83).

Left: Sculptured roof boss depicting Samson's victory over a lion (Judges 14), from Keynsham Abbey Somerset, UK.

As told in 1 Kings 17, Elijah is saved from hunger in the desert when he is fed by the ravens in this illustration from the book, *Old Testament Stories*, c.1880.

The prophets

Elijah

Elijah was a ninth-century prophet in Israel, BC who opposed Israel's evil kings Ahab, Ahaziah and Jehoram. He challenged the priests of the pagan god Baal on Mount Carmel to prove the power of their god, shaming Baal and his worshippers and honouring Israel's God. At the start of his ministry God sent ravens to feed him during a famine. He performed miracles and spoke God's word despite powerful opposition; and at the end of his life he did not die but was taken up into heaven in a whirlwind. In the New Testament Elijah is associated with John the Baptist's prophetic ministry (1 Kings 17–21; 2 Kings 1–2; Matthew 17; Mark 9; Luke 9; John 1).

Elisha

Having witnessed Elijah's ascent into heaven, Elisha was quickly recognized as his successor. Elisha initially suffered mockery and opposition, but under God's direction he was able to bring the Israelites victory against their enemies the Moabites. He performed miracles, giving a limitless supply of oil to a poor widow, raising a dead boy to life, healing leprosy and making an iron axe-head float (1 Kings 19; 2 Kings 2–13).

Isaiah

Isaiah was an eighth-century BC prophet in Judah whose prophecies are among those recorded in the book of Isaiah. He was called to become a prophet in the reign of Uzziah, seeing a vision of God's holiness and his own complete unworthiness. He advised King Ahaz politically and reassured King Hezekiah that the Assyrians would not conquer Jerusalem (2 Kings 19–20; Isaiah 1–39; Matthew 12–15; John 12).

Jeremiah

Prophesying in the years before the fall of Jerusalem, Jeremiah is often referred to as a prophet of doom. But although he took God's impending judgment seriously he also preserved a sense of hope in dark times because of his unswerving trust in God's covenant. Just before the exile Jeremiah was imprisoned by the king of Judah and then forced against his will to go to Egypt. His most famous prophecy spoke of the destruction of nations because of their idolatry, and took place at a potter's house, where Jeremiah was shown God's sovereignty over all that God had made, like the potter's control of his clay (2 Chronicles 35–36; Jeremiah; Matthew 2:17; 16:14; 27:9).

Ezekiel

Originally a priest, Ezekiel addressed his prophecies to the exiles in Babylon. He often acted out his visions, leading to some strange behaviour (including eating a scroll and lying on his side for long periods). He assured God's people that they had not been forgotten even in exile, and his detailed vision of the new Temple in Jerusalem inspired them with hope. His vision of a valley of dry bones powerfully expresses the idea that life and hope are totally dependent on God and not on human factors.

Daniel
(See chapter 4, **Daniel**)

Jonah
(See chapter 4, **Jonah**)

Haggai
(See chapter 4, **Haggai**)

Hosea
(See chapter 4, **Hosea**)

Zechariah
(See chapter 4, **Zechariah**)

Kings and queens

Saul

The first king of Israel, Saul, was anointed by Samuel and filled with the Spirit. In his youth Saul was already marked out by prophecies. He became king at the age of thirty and his reign was initially promising: he subdued the Israelites' enemies, including the Moabites, Ammonites, Edomites and Philistines. But Saul was disobedient to God's word and God

Jeremiah uses the metaphor of pottery to warn the house of Israel against idolatry (Jeremiah 18: 4–6). Illustration by William Hole (1846–1917).

Statue of Saul, Provence, France.

rejected him as king. A rather volatile character, Saul experienced mood swings and displayed unpredictable behaviour. He became envious of David's popularity and even tried to kill David. In his despair at God's rejection he consulted a witch about an impending battle with the Philistines. He was critically wounded in the battle and ended his own life (1 Samuel 9–31; 1 Chronicles 10).

David

Saul's successor, David, achieved great military victories and also led God's people in their religious life. God made a special covenant with David that established the importance of his royal line, from which the New Testament says that Jesus was descended. David's early life was spent in the service of Saul. He played the harp for him, but also defeated the Philistine giant Goliath. He became a close friend of Jonathan, Saul's son. David lived in Bethlehem and was looking after his father's sheep when Samuel the prophet came and anointed him as king at God's command. David's achievements included taking control of Jerusalem for the first time and making it Israel's capital, and bringing the Ark of the Covenant to the city. Although he was loved by God, he fell into sin, having an affair with Bathsheba, the wife of Uriah, and even ordering Uriah's death. The prophet Nathan brought God's judgment to David for what he had done, and the son born to David and Bathsheba died. David then repented of his sin and another son, Solomon, was born to

them. After further victories against the Philistines David anointed Solomon as king. David wrote many songs and prayers that reflected the ups and downs of his life. He died and was buried in Jerusalem, 'the City of David' (1 Samuel 16–30; 2 Samuel; 1 Kings 1–11; 1 Chronicles 11–29; Psalms; Matthew 11; Luke 1; Acts 2, 13).

Solomon

David's son and successor, Solomon, built the Temple at Jerusalem. Solomon's 39-year reign saw a period of peace and prosperity in Israel, and Jerusalem was firmly established at the centre of the nation's political and religious life. Although his wisdom and his wealth have become proverbial, Solomon was not always popular, especially with the people who suffered under his harsh taxation policies. His personal life reflected pagan legacies (he had a large harem, and made sacrifices to pagan gods) and God told him that the kingdom he established would not last long because of his lack of commitment to God's covenant. In fact it crumbled shortly after his death (1 Kings 1–11; 1 Chronicles 29; 2 Chronicles 1–9; Proverbs 1; Song of Songs; Matthew 1; 6:29; Luke 11:31; Acts 7:47).

Queen of Sheba

This queen from Arabia visited Solomon, possibly on a trade mission. She was impressed by his wisdom and prosperity. The queen gave Solomon spices, gold and precious stones, and Solomon gave her in return whatever she asked for. This foreign queen praised God for having appointed Solomon as king and for demonstrating God's eternal love for Israel (1 Kings 10; 2 Chronicles 9).

Esther

Esther was a young Jewish orphan girl, brought up by her uncle Mordecai. She rose from obscurity to become the wife of Xerxes, king of Persia. Her rise was due to God's providence (though this is not made explicit in the story), her own ability to win favour and Xerxes' desire for her. When a plot was discovered to wipe out all the Jewish people in the Persian empire, Esther risked her own life by revealing her Jewish roots and pleading with Xerxes on their behalf. To this day the Jewish people celebrate Esther's miraculous success at the festival of Purim. (See Esther 1–10; see chapter 4, **Esther**.)

Jesus and his family

(See also chapter 5, **Overview of the New Testament; Jesus' birth and early life.**)

Jesus

Jesus (whose name means 'the Lord saves') was born in Bethlehem and grew up in Nazareth. Little is known of his early life; his baptism in the Jordan marked the start

Left: Detail of the final panel from the *Gates of Paradise* by Lorenzo Ghiberti (1378–1455), in which Solomon greets the queen of Sheba in Jerusalem (1 Kings 10).

Right: Esther is depicted in this stained glass at St Mary's Church, Bury St Edmunds, Suffolk, UK.

of his public story. From the age of about thirty he travelled around the towns of Galilee, teaching, healing and performing other miracles, before extending his ministry to Jerusalem. He had no home of his own and relied on support from his friends and followers. He died the death of a criminal, crucified on a hill on the outskirts of Jerusalem. He was buried in a borrowed tomb, but appeared to his disciples after his death before ascending into heaven.

Mary and Joseph

Mary, the mother of Jesus, became pregnant while remaining a virgin according to the New Testament. Jesus was not the son of her husband, Joseph, but was conceived 'from the Holy Spirit'. Mary and Joseph were devout Jewish people who circumcised their son and went to Jerusalem annually for the feast of Passover. Joseph was a carpenter by trade, whose family line could be traced back to King David and Abraham. In the Gospels Mary's faith is emphasized by her acceptance of her role in Jesus' birth, her prophetic song (known as the Magnificat), her presence at Jesus' crucifixion and her presence with the apostles after Jesus' resurrection. Jesus showed obedience towards his parents and care for his mother even from the cross. It seems that Joseph died some time before Jesus did (Matthew 1–2; Luke 2; John 19:26–27; Acts 1:14).

Jesus' siblings

No sisters of Jesus are named in the New Testament, but James, Joseph, Simon and Jude (Judas) are described as his brothers. The Roman Catholic Church holds that Mary remained a virgin throughout her life, so Catholics regard Jesus' so-called siblings as cousins or half-siblings, a possible interpretation of the Greek word used in the Gospels. Jesus' close family did not fully understand the nature of his ministry, especially in its early days, although they showed concern for his well-being. Jesus' brothers joined in prayer with the first Christians and were held in great respect by the early church. James, who saw the risen Christ, subsequently led the church in Jerusalem (taking charge at the Council of Jerusalem) and wrote the letter of James. Jude wrote the New Testament letter bearing his name (Matthew 13:55–56; Mark 3:20–21, 31–35; John 7:1–13; Acts 1:14; 15; 1 Corinthians 15:7).

Jesus' wider family

Among Jesus' other relatives were Zechariah, a priest, and his wife Elizabeth, who were the parents of John the Baptist. Mary stayed with them for three months before Jesus was born. Zechariah was unable to speak from the time when the angel Gabriel appeared to him announcing John's birth until the baby was actually born, because he did not believe that he would have a son. At John's birth he prophesied John's ministry in a song known as the Benedictus (Luke 1: 5–80).

John the Baptist

Jesus identified John the Baptist as a prophet, a second Elijah. He wore clothes

forerunners of all those people throughout the centuries who have followed Jesus. During Jesus' lifetime these twelve were the 'inner circle', accompanying Jesus at the most important moments of his life. They had no particular qualifications and were sometimes slow to understand, but it is to them that Jesus committed the future of the church.

Mary, Joseph and Jesus travel to Egypt (Matthew 2:13–15), as depicted by William Hole (1846–1917).

Peter (Simon)

Originally a fisherman known as Simon, Peter was so named by Jesus ('the rock' – Aramaic 'Cephas', in Greek, 'Peter') when he recognized Jesus as the messiah. Peter often acted as spokesperson for the disciples and, although he denied Jesus after Jesus was arrested, he was commissioned by Jesus in a resurrection appearance to carry on the Christian ministry. On the day of Pentecost Peter encouraged Jewish people to have faith in Jesus, and over 3,000 people became Christians. Peter also took the Christian message to the Gentiles. His ministry led to many healing miracles and conversions, as well as to his own imprisonment. It was Peter who baptized the first Gentile converts, Cornelius and his household. He became the leader of the church in Jerusalem and wrote 1 and 2 Peter. Later tradition associated Peter with both Antioch and Rome, and from the second century onwards the leader of the church at Rome traced his own authority to that of Peter. (Matthew 16:13–20; Mark 10:28; 14:27–42; 66–72; Luke 22: 31–34, 54, 62; John 1:40–42; 21; Acts 2:14–41;

of camel hair and lived an ascetic lifestyle. John prepared the way for Jesus; his ministry was characterized by no-nonsense preaching about the need for repentance and baptism with water. John baptized people in the Jordan – including Jesus. He was imprisoned and then beheaded by Herod (Matthew 3; 11; 14; Mark 1; 6; Luke 1; 3; 7; 9; John 1–5, 10; Acts 1, 11; 13).

The twelve disciples

Jesus called twelve men from a variety of backgrounds (fishermen, tax collectors, zealots) to follow him. They responded to his call, left their livelihoods and families behind, learned from Jesus and submitted themselves to his teaching. They were the

Detail from a bronze relief of Jesus and the Twelve at the Last Supper. Taken from a holy communion box at the St Mary of Zion New Church, Axum, Ethiopia.

John (son of Zebedee)
John was the brother of James and another fisherman. He supported Peter in his early ministry and later became a leader of the churches in Jerusalem and Ephesus. (See Acts 3:1, 4, 11; 4:13, 19; 8:14.)

Philip
Philip came from Bethsaida, and was instrumental in introducing Nathanael to Jesus. He was a good friend of Andrew. (John 1:43–51; John 6:7; 12:22)

Nathanael (Bartholomew)
Not much is known about this disciple, although Jesus commended him as a true Israelite and Nathanael recognized Jesus from the start as the Son of God. (Mark 3:18; John 1:43–51; Acts 1:13–14.)

3:1 – 5:42; 10–12.) (See chapter 6, **Apostles and leaders of the church**, below.)

Andrew
Andrew was the brother of Peter and originally a disciple of John the Baptist. He introduced Peter to Jesus and together they left their jobs as fishermen to follow Jesus. He was active alongside the other apostles in the early church. (John 1:35–42; 6:8–9; 12:22; Acts 1:13–14.)

James (son of Zebedee)
James was also from a fishing family and became one of Jesus' most trusted friends. He was martyred for his faith. (See Mark 10:35; Acts 12:2.)

Thomas (Didymus, 'the twin')
Thomas is often called 'the doubter' because when he saw the risen Jesus he would not believe until he could touch Jesus' wounded side. But having done so he made a bold declaration of faith. (John 11:16; 20:24–29.)

Matthew (Levi)
Matthew left his job as a tax-collector to follow Jesus and held a banquet in Jesus' honour. (Matthew 9:9–13; Luke 5:27–32.)

James (son of Alphaeus)
This James can probably be identified with 'James the younger', whose mother was present at the crucifixion. (Mark 15:40; Luke 6:15.)

Simon the Zealot

The epithet 'Zealot' probably indicates Simon's allegiance to a Jewish militant group, although it was also used more generally to describe people with a zealous commitment to the history and preservation of the Israelite faith. (See chapter 7, **Nations and groups in the Bible**.) (Matthew 10:4; Luke 6:15.)

Judas (son of James)

Judas was probably the Thaddaeus of Mark's Gospel. (John 14:22; Luke 6:16.)

Judas Iscariot

The disciple who betrayed Jesus. He was paid money (thirty pieces of silver), but fear, criticism, human weakness, misunderstanding and his own ideas about the expected messiah all had their place in leading him towards betrayal. Afterwards he committed suicide, according to Matthew's Gospel, suggesting that he felt regret. He was replaced by Matthias. (See Matthew 26:14–16, 47–51; 27:3–10; John 6:67–70; 12:1–8; 13:21–30; Acts 1:15–26.)

People who met Jesus

Jesus spent time with individuals as well as large crowds. In particular he broke down social barriers as he mixed with Samaritans, tax-collectors, rich people, poor people, well-known political and religious leaders as well as numerous women. In the table below, some of his most important encounters are listed.

Jesus meets poor people	Blind Bartimaeus (Mark 10:46–52) Widow at Nain Luke (7:11–17) Invalid at the pool of Bethesda (John 5)
Jesus meets rich people	Rich young man (Mark 10:17–31) Zacchaeus (Luke 19:1–10) Royal official with a sick son (John 4:43–54)
Jesus meets the outcasts of society	A man with leprosy (Mark 1:40–45; Luke 5:12–14) Possessed man near Gerasa (Mark 5:1–20; Luke 8:26–39)
Jesus meets Samaritans and women	Syro-Phoenician woman (Mark 7:24–30) Samaritan woman at the well (John 4) Mary and Martha (Luke 10:38–42)
Jesus meets religious leaders	Nicodemus (John 3) Caiaphas the high priest (Matthew 26:57–68; John 18:19–24)
Jesus meets political leaders	Centurion at Capernaum (Matthew 8:5–13; Mark 7:1–10) Pilate (and Herod) (Matthew 27:19–26; Mark 15:1–15; Luke 22:26–23:25; John 18:29–19:38)

Illustration of Jesus sitting in front of a well and asking a Samaritan woman to fill the bowl with water from the pitcher (John 4).

Apostles and leaders of the church

(For **Peter, James, and Philip** see **The twelve disciples**, above.)

Barnabas
Barnabas, a Levite from Cyprus, was a friend and colleague of Paul. He commended Paul to the Christians at Jerusalem and later on travelled with him, boldly preaching the gospel. Barnabas was influential in the churches in Antioch and Jerusalem. He separated from Paul over a disagreement, but Paul continued to respect him. The name Barnabas (meaning 'son of encouragement') was given to him by the apostles. (Acts 4:36; 9:26–27; 13:1–5, 42–52; 14; 1 Corinthians 9:6.)

John Mark
John Mark was Barnabas's cousin, who accompanied Paul and Barnabas for part of their first missionary journey. He left them early to return to Jerusalem, so Paul decided to leave him behind when he set off on his second mission. Nevertheless John Mark was not sidelined by Paul: Paul asked him to come and help during his imprisonment in Rome. John Mark was also a friend of Peter, and is probably the author of Mark's Gospel. (Acts 15:36–41; Colossians 4:10; 2 Timothy 4:11; Philemon 24.)

Paul
Paul (originally known by his Hebrew name, Saul) was a Pharisee and persecutor of Christians. But he became a Christian after being struck blind on the Damascus road and seeing a vision of the risen Christ. After some years in Galatia and then preaching in Damascus and Jerusalem, Paul embarked on a travelling ministry. He founded and then led many Christian churches along the Mediterranean coast, writing numerous letters to stay in contact with them when he left. After a period of imprisonment in Caesarea, he was sent to Rome to be tried as a Roman citizen, where he once again endured imprisonment and house arrest. He was probably executed just outside Rome during the reign of Nero. (Acts 9; 13–28.) (See chapter 5, **Letters in the New Testament**.)

Philip the evangelist
Philip came from Caesarea, and was a successful evangelist in Samaria (where

Simon the Sorcerer was converted). He also spoke about Jesus with an Ethiopian official who became a Christian and was baptized. Philip was one of the seven men appointed as deacons, whose duty was to look after food distribution to the poor. (Acts 6:1–7; 8; 21:8.)

Stephen

Stephen was an early Christian renowned for his faith and his inspiration by the Holy Spirit. He was also one of the seven deacons who were set apart to assist the apostles. He aroused opposition from Jewish leaders and delivered a remarkable sermon to the Sanhedrin council (see chapter 7, **Jewish groups**). Stephen was the first Christian martyr, stoned to death for his faith. Saul, not yet a convert, was present in the crowd at his stoning. (Acts 6 and 7.)

Timothy

Timothy had a Greek father, but his mother, Eunice, was a Jewish Christian, as was his grandmother Lois. Paul took Timothy on mission with him and trained him in pastoral ministry. He served with Paul in Corinth and then led the church that Paul founded in Ephesus. Like Paul, he suffered imprisonment for his faith. The two affectionate New Testament letters, 1 and 2 Timothy, may have been written to him by Paul to encourage him and advise him about how he should develop his gifts and care for the churches where he ministered, although some scholars today believe that they were

The apostle Philip baptizes the eunuch (Acts 8), 16th century.

written later. (See chapter 5, **Pastoral Epistles.**) (Acts 16:1–2; 17:14–15; 19:22; 1 Corinthians 4:17; 16:10–11; Philippians 2:19–22; 1 Thessalonians 3:2, 6–7; 1 and 2 Timothy; Hebrews 13:23.)

Titus

Titus accompanied Paul and Barnabas to Jerusalem and was an important helper to Paul in Corinth. In the epistle to Titus, again traditionally but not certainly attributed to Paul, he is serving as the leader of the church in Crete, which

Jesus in the house of Martha and Mary (Luke 10), an illustration from the book, *The Life of Our Lord*, c.1880.

involves some pioneering work. (2 Corinthians 7:14–15; 8:16–24; Titus.)

Women in the Bible

Eve
(See **Adam and Eve**, above.)

The wives of the patriarchs
(See **Abraham, Isaac, Jacob**, above.)

Deborah
(See **The leaders and judges**, above.)

Ruth and Naomi
(See chapter 4, **Book of Ruth**.)

Hannah
(See Samuel, above.)

Mary Magdalene
One of the women who travelled with and supported Jesus and his disciples, Mary had been healed from possession by a demon. On the day after Jesus' crucifixion she visited Jesus' tomb, saw that the tombstone had been removed and called Peter and another disciple (probably John). She wept at the tomb entrance, and then the risen Jesus addressed her personally by name. Mary reported to the disciples, 'I have seen the Lord.' She has traditionally been regarded as a repentant sinner, although there is no evidence for this in the Bible text. (See Luke 8:2; John 20:1–18.)

Mary and Martha
Mary and Martha were sisters from Bethany who welcomed Jesus as their guest. Jesus intervened in a dispute between them when Martha complained that, while she was busy working, her sister simply sat at Jesus' feet listening to him. When their brother Lazarus fell ill, the sisters sent word to Jesus, but by the time Jesus arrived Lazarus had died. Jesus wept, but then he summoned Lazarus from the grave back to life again. Jesus was very attentive towards these two women, and the Gospels tell us that he loved this family. Mary showed her love for Jesus when she anointed him by pouring perfume over him. (Luke 10:38–42; John 11:1–44.)

Sapphira

Sapphira was the wife of Ananias who, along with her husband, sought to deceive the apostles about money they were donating from the sale of a field, keeping some of it back for themselves. Both died suddenly when their fraud was discovered. (Acts 5:1–11.)

Lydia

Lydia was a seller of purple cloth who lived in Philippi and responded to Paul's ministry. She and her household were baptized; she provided hospitality for Paul and his companions, and believers met in her home. (Acts 16:11–15, 40.)

Priscilla

Priscilla was the wife of Aquila, and both were close friends of Paul. They gave Paul hospitality and hosted a house church. (Acts 18:1–3; Romans 16:3; 1 Corinthians 16:19.)

Further reading suggestions

Paul Gardner (ed), *The Complete Who's Who of the Bible*, London, Marshall, Pickering, 1995.

7

Nations and Groups in the Bible

The twelve tribes of Israel

The twelve tribes of Israel are traditionally regarded as descending from Jacob's twelve sons. Following the successful campaigns of Joshua's armies after the Israelites entered the Promised Land (Canaan) they each held different territories, but it is likely that they formed an 'association of tribes' as other ancient communities did. In other words, they shared a corporate life involving a central shrine, an annual festival and the defence of common interests. In the Old Testament we see many examples of tribes joining together in the face of a common threat from outside or within (for example, six tribes united with Deborah against the Canaanites and eleven joined forces to denounce the sin of the Benjaminites). Jacob's and Moses' words of blessing on the tribes are recorded in Genesis 49 and Deuteronomy 33. (See chapter 6, **Patriarchs, Jacob**.)

Asher

The tribe of Asher occupied a coastal region north of Mount Carmel nearly 100 km (60 miles) long. Its location brought close contact with the trading Phoenicians.

Bas-relief from the throne room of Nebuchadnezzar in Babylon, c. 604–562 BC.

Moses pronounced a blessing on Asher, usually understood as referring to its military strength, but it never managed to drive out the Canaanites from its cities. Anna (Luke 2:36) was a member of this tribe. Asher is regarded as deriving from Jacob's second son with Leah's servant.

Benjamin

Although the tribe of Benjamin had the smallest amount of territory (less than 50 km or 30 miles long), this territory was significant in that it contained Jerusalem, Bethel and Kiriath Jearim. The tribe was promised God's protection and favour by Jacob. The Benjaminites were known for their skill in warfare, especially in using the bow and the sling. The tribe of Benjamin was massacred by the other tribes after a Benjaminite mob raped the mistress of a Levite, but it was not wiped out. It eventually united with the tribe of Simeon and became part of Judah. King David and the apostle Paul were descended from this tribe, which derives from Jacob's last son with his wife Rachel. (Judges 20–21; 1 Samuel 20:20; 2 Samuel 1:22.)

Dan

The tribe of Dan derives from Jacob's son with Rachel's servant, Bilhah. The tribe settled first in the central part of Canaan, but moved northwards to Laish following opposition from the Amorites. The tribe rebuilt this city and renamed it Dan; it is mentioned sometimes in the Old Testament almost as shorthand for the northern border of the Promised Land. One of the

craftsmen involved in constructing the tabernacle, Oholiab, was from this tribe, as was Samson.

Gad

Gad was the first son of Leah's servant, Zilpah. The tribe named after him was relatively small; it settled east of the Jordan in southern Gilead. Its main occupation was keeping livestock and its land was bordered by hostile powers, including the Syrians and the Ammonites. When the tribes east of the Jordan were transported to Assyria in the mid eighth century BC the Ammonites occupied their land.

Issachar

Issachar was a hard-working tribe that settled between the tribes of Zebulun and Manasseh/Ephraim, south of the Sea of Galilee and west of the Jordan. Part of its territory was the fertile plain of Jezreel, which provided good crops – but these were often looted, as the area remained a Canaanite stronghold. Deborah and Barak were from this tribe and Deborah commended it for its part in the campaign against Sisera. (See Judges 5:15; 1 Chronicles 32:38.)

Joseph (Ephraim/Manasseh)

Joseph was given a double share in the tribes of Israel because, in one of his last actions, Jacob adopted Joseph's two sons – Jacob's grandsons – as his own. So two Israelite tribes were descended from Joseph: Ephraim and Manasseh. Ephraim occupied the southern territory of the Northern Kingdom, west of the Jordan (incorporating Shiloh and Shechem, with Bethel on its southern border). Jeroboam, who rebelled against the rule of Solomon's son Rehoboam and established the Northern Kingdom, was from this tribe. Other leaders included Joshua and Samuel. The tribe of Manasseh straddled the Jordan in the central territory of the Northern Kingdom, exposed to attacks from the Arameans and Assyrians. Gideon and Jephthah were among its leaders.

Judah

Judah's descendants were singled out for special blessing by Jacob. It was the first tribe to take possession of its land, located in the southern area of the Promised Land, between the territories of Philistia and Moab. During the time of the judges Judah was involved in constant battles with the Philistines, but it became the most important tribe and occupied about a third of the whole land. Caleb, who went to spy out the land of Canaan, was from this tribe, and Jesus himself was descended from it.

Levi

The tribe of Levi had no territory but was scattered across the Promised Land, occupying forty-eight cities, six of which were cities of refuge (See chapter 8, **Cities of refuge**.) It became responsible for the worship life of Israel and was known as the priestly tribe. The other tribes were responsible for providing for their needs. The tribe was descended from Jacob and his first wife, Leah.

Naphtali

The second son of Rachel's servant was the ancestor of the tribe of Naphtali. It occupied land towards the north of the Sea of Galilee and established nineteen fortified cities. Its territory was in a favourable position, with good water supplies and rich soils. Trade links to Egypt ran along its borders. Despite its natural resources it was vulnerable to Syrian and Assyrian invasion, and Tiglath-Pileser III took over the region in 733 BC. Isaiah, however, prophesied that a great light would shine in the darkness: Jesus' Galilean ministry took place in the territory of Naphtali.

Reuben

Although the tribe of Reuben traced its origins to Jacob's firstborn son, its prominence faded along with its size. Reuben occupied the territory north of the River Arnon, but east of the Jordan, so it was physically separated from the stronger tribes. It seems eventually to have merged with Gad, to the north. It had the advantage of trade routes passing through its territory but this also meant that it was open to attack from enemies. The Moabites occupied its towns by the ninth century BC, and the Assyrian Tiglath-Pileser III took its last leader into exile. (1 Chronicles 5:6; 2 Chronicles 5:10, 18–22.)

Simeon

Simeon was a small tribe in the south, not even mentioned when Moses blessed the tribes. It became absorbed into the tribe of Judah, and its cities soon began to be called cities of Judah. (Joshua 15; 1 Chronicles 4.)

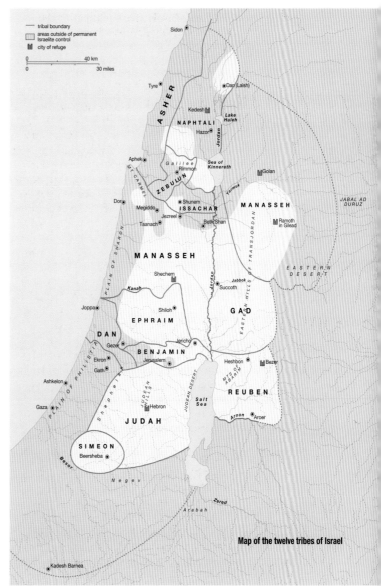

Map of the twelve tribes of Israel

An Assyrian stele depicting the storm-god Baal with a thunderbolt, from Ugarit (Ras Shamra), c. 1350–1250 BC.

Zebulun

Often mentioned alongside Issachar because of their close geographical proximity, Zebulun occupied the Galilean hill territory to the south of the Sea of Galilee, west of the Jordan. Nazareth and Cana were located within this territory. The tribe was celebrated for its righteousness and probably set up Mount Tabor as a centre for worship. Its territory is mentioned in the prophecy of Isaiah 9 along with that of Naphtali. During the expansion of the Assyrian Tiglath-Pileser III, Zebulun's population was deported and its territory was added to Assyrian land. (See Isaiah 9; Matthew 4:12–17.)

Other nations

Arameans

This nation of nomadic farmers came to prominence after the eleventh century BC. They are mentioned in Samuel, Kings and Chronicles. During the period of the kings, Israel was troubled by wars with the Arameans (probably the same people known as 'Syrians').

Assyrians

The Assyrians, a Semitic people with strong Babylonian influences, were based in what is now northern Iraq, to the north-east of the Northern Kingdom, and emerged around 1500 BC.

They were responsible for the fall of the city of Samaria in 722 BC, and controlled Judah for many years too, following Ahaz's submission to them. The Assyrians eventually dominated the whole region, including Egypt, and made Nineveh their cultural centre, establishing a royal library there. They were cruel oppressors but were defeated by the Babylonians, who took all their main cities including Nineveh (612 BC).

Babylonians

The Babylonians established the city of Babylon as the centre of their large territory (now Iraq) at the head of the Persian Gulf, south of Mesopotamia. The Israelites were exiled to Babylonia for fifty years, and although the Bible witnesses its wealth and prosperity they longed to return home. The Babylonians were well known for their many gods; their chief deity was Marduk. Babylon became a symbol of worldly power, in opposition to God's power, in the prophetic period, but when Babylon was taken over by the Persian king Cyrus in 539 BC its independence came to an end. Revelation uses Babylon as a symbol of the oppressive power of Rome. There is much archaeological evidence from Babylon demonstrating varied cultural life and religious activity. (See chapter 2, **Archaeology, Enuma Elish** and **Gilgamesh epic.**)

Canaanites

This label is used to designate the people who occupied the Promised Land when the Israelites arrived there – Amorites, Hittites, Girgashites, Perizzites, Hivites and Jebusites. Before the arrival of the Israelites, Canaan was organized around its cities, each with its own leaders. Its fertile land supplied the needs of its population. The Egyptians controlled Canaan from early in the second millennium BC, having realized Canaan's strategic position on major trade routes. Once Egypt's power faded in Canaan, the land was divided between different groups of people, including the Israelites and the Philistines. However, the pagan religion of the Canaanites endured for many years afterwards and Israelite prophets continued to warn their people against the temptation of following Canaanite gods, including Baal.

Egyptians

The Egyptians occupied the land surrounding the River Nile and were a formidable force from 3000 to 100 BC. Although it was associated with the persecution of the Israelites in the time of Moses, Egypt first appears in the Bible as the place where Joseph came to prominence and where his family settled to escape famine. In Old Testament times, Egypt was known as an advanced culture, but its power declined from around 1200 BC. Even so, the Israelites often turned to Egypt when other nations threatened them.

Greeks

Alexander the Great brought the eastern Mediterranean region under Greek control

Egyptian relief, from an exhibition at the Louvre in Paris, France.

between 334 and 323 BC. He overcame the Persians and established a new city in Egypt in his own honour, Alexandria, which soon became populated by Jewish communities. The tensions that arose through the subsequent meeting of Greek and Jewish cultures led to the Maccabean revolt. The Greeks were a great trading nation, using sea routes to generate wealth. Greek quickly became the *lingua franca* of the ancient world. Corinth and Athens were important centres of Greek culture and commerce. (See chapter 5, **The New Testament story**.)

Hittites

Occupying the land south of the Black Sea in Asia Minor (now Turkey), the Hittites are mentioned in Genesis as living around

The caves at Qumran where the Dead Sea scrolls were discovered in 1946.

the city of Hebron in Abraham's time. They are mentioned again among the peoples occupying the Promised Land when the Israelites arrived there. They were reasonably prominent from 1600 to 1200 BC. (Genesis 15:19; 1 Chronicles 1:13; 1 Kings 11:1; 2 Kings 7:7–6.)

Medes and Persians

The Medes and Persians became linked together after King Cyrus of Persia overthrew the Medes in 549 BC. Cyrus then conquered the Babylonians in 539 BC and allowed the Jewish exiles to return to their homeland. Then he, and his successor Darius I, financed the rebuilding of their temples and cities. Cyrus ruled over most of the Old Testament world once the Babylonians were defeated, and Aramaic became the common language across the Persian empire.

Midianites

Midianite tradesmen were among the merchants who took Joseph off to Egypt as a slave. They were a desert people, living in tents and leading a nomadic existence. When Moses fled from Egypt he travelled north to Midian where he met Jethro, who became his father-in-law. Jethro is described as 'a priest of Midian'. It appears that the Midianites opposed the Israelites for at least seven years. (See Exodus 2:16; Judges 6–7.)

Philistines

The Philistines occupied the coastal land of the former Canaanite territory, to the south of Israel and west of Judah. They established the five cities of Ekron, Ashdod, Ashkelon, Gath and Gaza as centres of power and eventually gave their name to the whole area they occupied (Palestine). Samson, Samuel, Saul and David were involved in hostile encounters with the Philistines, but only David overcame them. They became representative in the Old Testament of enmity towards God's people and the lure of pagan worship.

New Testament Jewish groups

Essenes

Evidence for the existence of this Jewish monastic community comes from the discovery of the Dead Sea scrolls at Qumran in 1946.

It seems that other members of this religious group were based in towns and sought to influence mainstream Judaism. All had in common a desire to be pure and to be ready for God's anticipated intervention to save God's people in a dramatic historical moment when the messiah (or messiahs: one royal and one priestly) would come. The Essenes strongly believed that the faithful members of their community were the true inheritors of the promises of God to Israel. The name 'Essenes' was not used by the group itself but by others and probably relates to the idea of piety. The centre of Essene life at Qumran was destroyed by the armies of the future Roman emperor Vespasian (c. AD 68), but the documents regulating the life of this community (the Dead Sea scrolls) were stored safely in libraries in surrounding caves. (See chapter 2, **Dead Sea scrolls**.)

Scribes and Pharisees

Present in most Palestinian towns in the time of Jesus and numbering about 6,000, the Pharisees were the intellectual class responsible for leading the religious activities of the Jewish people. The group probably emerged as early as the second century BC. They were especially respected for their scholarship and understanding of the Old Testament Law.

The term 'Pharisee' means 'separated one', and their primary concern was to separate themselves from all impurity. Some Pharisees were full-time scholars, others combined their study with different professions; but all were concerned to protect the Law by producing other rules and regulations to help prevent its being violated. In this sense they were radicals and were critical of the religious establishment. Jesus encountered particular opposition from this group. He did not give these Jewish teachers the respect that other people showed them; in fact he called them hypocrites. Jesus

The Pharisees Question Jesus (1886–94) illustrates Matthew 22, by James Tissot.

found that some Pharisees did not practise what they preached. He reminded them that the essence of the Law was God's love for God's people. Instead of being used to protect God's people, Jesus argued that the law had become a noose around their necks, sometimes even preventing their lives from being saved. Paul the apostle was a Pharisee (see Philippians 3:6; Romans 7:14–15; 1 Timothy 1:15) and, after his conversion to Christianity, he was well placed to explain the place of the Law to the followers of Jesus.

Associated with the Pharisees is the group known as 'the scribes'. They are described by the Gospel writers as 'teachers of the law' and operated almost everywhere (see Luke 5:17). Their job was literally to preserve the Law by ensuring it was copied accurately, but they also taught the Law along with all the interpretations and oral traditions associated with it. They were paid for these services as well as for making judgments based on the Law.

Priests and Levites

Because of the centrality of the Temple in Jewish religious life, the families of priests based in Jerusalem were wealthy in the time of Jesus. The priests were subject to special rules of ritual purity. The appointment of high priests was already a matter of political concern and while the high priests had a measure of influence over figures of authority, they were also subject to their demands. The high priests wore elaborate clothes for the special festival occasions when they would appear in the Temple.

The Levites fulfilled practical roles in the Temple on a daily basis, for example dealing with daily offerings.

Sadducees

The Sadducees were the religious conservatives of their day. They did not want changes in religious practice and, although few in number, they were influential, which probably had something to do with their connections to Jerusalem's high society. They held to a literal understanding of the Pentateuch, the only part of the Old Testament they considered authoritative. They did not see a need to reinterpret it in the light of new circumstances; neither did they believe in the afterlife or a spiritual world of demons and angels. Both these views brought them into conflict with the Pharisees, although in the New Testament the two groups are sometimes considered together (see, for example, Matthew 3:7ff). It was the Sadducees who appeared most disturbed by the teaching of Peter and John in Acts and who put them in prison at least twice (Acts 4 and 5).

Samaritans

This group of Israelite origin were considered traitors by most Jews in New Testament times. It is thought that their history may be associated with Sanballat and Tobiah, who represented a mixed community that collaborated with foreign rulers and admitted mixed marriages during the Babylonian exile (Nehemiah 13:27–28). Their descendants suffered ridicule from mainstream Judaism for a perceived lack of integrity and loyalty. Their insistence that only the Pentateuch was authoritative and that Mount Gerizim was the true place of worship brought them into further disagreement with mainstream Judaism. Jesus demonstrated a special interest in this persecuted group, talking with a Samaritan woman and using Samaritans as examples in his parables (see Luke 4, 10, 17; John 4). The apostles in the early church period preached the gospel to Samaritan people and found them receptive to it (see Acts 8). (See chapter 6, **People Jesus met** and chapter 8, **Mount Gerizim**).

Sanhedrin

This was the name of the courts or councils that were responsible for regulating Jewish life at an official level, including handling the trials of individuals accused of breaking religious laws or being politically subversive. The Sanhedrin that gathered in the Temple in Jerusalem was the highest court, but many other Sanhedrin councils met in other major cities. The Temple Sanhedrin was not regulated by the Roman authorities and was concerned only with religious law. The Sanhedrin is mentioned in the stories about the trial of Jesus in the Gospels. Because Jesus was viewed as a messianic pretender, he would have troubled those with both political and religious jurisdiction.

Zealots

While similar to the Pharisees in their religious views, this group had a different attitude to the Roman authorities. Rather than seeking to work alongside them, the Zealots were militants in the first century and were determined to drive out the Romans. This commitment was clearly related to their belief that state rulers represented a barrier to the sole worship of God. For this reason they also refused to pay taxes. At least one of Jesus' disciples was a Zealot (see Chapter 6, **Simon**). The actions of the Zealots in promoting Jewish revolt led to the fall of Jerusalem, when it was taken by the Romans in AD 70.

New Testament culture

Greeks
(See chapter 5, **the New Testament story**; and above **Greeks**.)

Entrance to the ancient tombs of the Sanhedrin. In Temple times the Sanhedrin was the high court of seventy-one sages who issued decisions regarding Jewish laws.

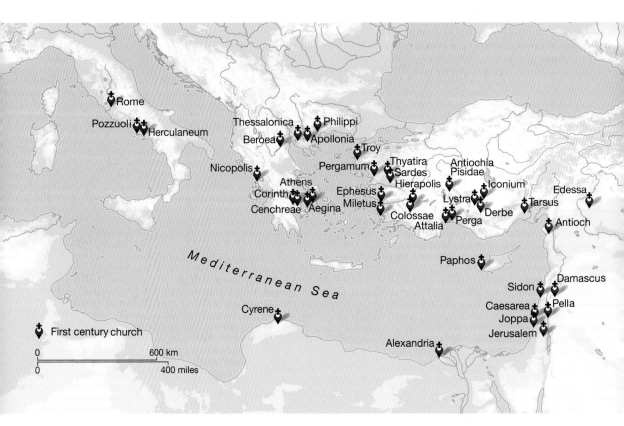

Map of the 1st-century AD Roman empire.

Romans

The Roman republic became an empire under Augustus Caesar in 27 BC. By New Testament times it had conquered most of the Near East, including Syria and Egypt, and therefore provides the context for the New Testament events in terms of culture, politics and location. Most of the empire consisted of provinces under Roman governors, but some regions, such as Judea at the time of Jesus' birth, were, in the short term, left under local kings. Roman society was immensely influenced by Greek culture – the Greek language serving as the clearest example of its lasting influence. But the intellectual pursuits of the Greeks had also aroused a hunger to know truth and to gain answers about the world. As a result a political agenda emerged among the Jews that viewed Roman rule as an unwelcome presence. The Jewish population also had its influence on Roman society and there

were synagogues in most Roman cities.
In the period after the resurrection, the
church spread to Rome itself, not least
because of the efforts of the apostle Paul, a
Romanized Jew who laid some stress on his
status as a Roman citizen. (See chapter 2,
Geography.)

8

Places in the Bible

Places where people meet God

Although people encounter God in many different locations in the Bible, the places listed here have been selected because they have become well known as places of encounter with God.

Deserts

Desert of Judah: Jesus went into the desert following his baptism and in preparation for his ministry. This was probably in the Judean desert area. He was tempted there by Satan, but found God able to sustain him. (See Matthew 4:1–11; Mark 1:12–13; Luke 4:1–13.)

The Judean desert.

Desert spring on the road to Shur: when Hagar, Abraham's slave and mistress, fled from his home she met God at a spring in the desert. She called God 'the God who sees me' in recognition that God was aware of her distress. (See Genesis 16.)

Gardens

Eden: God placed Adam and then Eve (see chapter 6, **Adam and Eve**) in a beautiful garden in Eden. It was here that they fell into sin and then heard God calling to them. They were led out of the garden as a consequence of their disobedience. Eden may have been located in Iraq or eastern Syria, as seems probable since it is described as having two rivers, which could be identified with the Tigris and Euphrates. Metaphorically, Eden represents the perfection before sin entered the world.(Genesis 2–3.)

Gethsemane: this garden has a name meaning 'oil press', probably relating to the fact that olives were grown there. Jesus went there to pray following his Last Supper with his disciples, before he was crucified. Jesus went to Gethsemane to be alone with his Father at the time of his greatest need, leading to agonizing prayer. It was in this place also that Judas betrayed Jesus. (See Matthew 26:25–46; Mark 14:32–42; Luke 22:40–46.)

Mountains
In biblical times mountains symbolized strength, the stability of the created order and the presence of God.

Gerizim and Ebal: these are two mountains that form a pass where Joshua led the people of Israel in a ceremony to renew their covenant with God. Joshua, following Moses' instructions, built an altar on Mount Ebal. In Jesus' time Samaritan people worshipped God on Mount Gerizim rather than in Jerusalem. (See Joshua 8:33; John 4:19.)

Mount of Olives: this is part of the mountain range that runs through the central and southern part of Palestine and is located east of Jerusalem. Jesus went there to teach his disciples and to withdraw from the crowds. The Gospels suggest that Jesus found peace and solitude to pray on the Mount of Olives. And Acts says that Jesus appeared to some of his disciples there following his resurrection and before he ascended into heaven.

(Matthew 24–25; 26:30; Luke 19:37–41; John 8:1; Acts 1:11.)

Sinai (Horeb): on this mountain God revealed himself to Moses in a burning bush and the people of Israel entered into their covenant with God. It was here that God gave Moses the Ten Commandments and other laws. God also appeared to the prophet Elijah on this mountain and his presence was accompanied by wind, earthquake and fire. (Exodus 3; 1 Kings 19:8–12.)

Rivers

Jabbok: this stream runs into the River Jordan and marks the boundary between the lands of the Ammonites and Gileadites. It was here that Jacob encountered God on his way back to meet his brother Esau. Here Jacob wrestled with God, received God's blessing and was given the new name 'Israel'. (Genesis 32:22–29.)

Towns and cities

Bethel: Bethel was an important city in Old Testament times, originally called Luz. Abraham built an altar there to God but it was Jacob who gave it the name Bethel (meaning 'house of God') after he had a dream there of a ladder reaching up to heaven with angels moving up and down it. Jacob declared: 'the Lord is in this place...

How awesome is this place.' From that time on Bethel was an important religious centre, rivalling the status of Jerusalem. It was situated on a major trade route between the lands of the Benjaminites and the Ephraimites. (Genesis 12:8; 28:19; Judges 20:18; 1 Samuel 7:16.)

Shiloh: Shiloh was another important religious centre that first came to prominence when Joshua led his campaigns from there. During the period of the judges the tabernacle was kept at Shiloh. Samuel was dedicated in the temple there. Shiloh was also designated a 'city of refuge' (see **Cities of refuge**). (Joshua 18–22; 1 Samuel 1.)

Places of God's miraculous intervention

Some places in the world of the Bible are particularly well known because stories about God's miraculous intervention are set in them.

Elah Valley: this was a fertile valley west of Bethlehem where David killed the Philistine champion Goliath. David told Goliath that this battle was the Lord's and, against all odds, killed him with a single stone from a slingshot. (1 Samuel 17.)

Jericho: Jericho was a major fortified city which the Israelites conquered under Joshua. Following God's instruction they walked around its walls for seven days, after which the walls miraculously collapsed. The moment that the city fell, Joshua acknowledged God's hand in this victory commanding the people: 'Shout! For the Lord has given you the city!' (Joshua 5:13 – 6:27.)

Mount Carmel: this mountain, located on the east coast of the Mediterranean Sea, was the place where the contest between the prophets of Baal and Elijah took place (see

chapter 6, **Elijah**). When the fire of the Lord descended on Elijah's altar the people respond by recognizing God's intervention and declaring that Elijah's God was Lord. (1 Kings 18:16–40.)

Mount Moriah: Moriah is the mountain region, three days' journey from Beersheba, where Abraham went to offer his son Isaac as a sacrifice (see chapter 6, **Abraham**) when God chose to test

Top left: The valley of Elah where David slew Goliath (1 Samuel 17).

Top right: Aerial view over modern-day refugee camps in Jericho.

Left: The Wadi Me'arot cave on Mount Carmel, contains evidence of inhabitation by prehistoric human beings continuously for 200,000 years, including: Acheulian cultures (150–200,000 years ago), Muarian cultures (100–150,000 years ago), Mousterian cultures (40–100,000 years ago), Uriniacian cultures (12–40,000 years ago), and Natufian cultures (12–19,000 years ago).

Top left: Tower of Babel (Genesis 11) by Pieter Brueghel the Elder, c. 1563.

Top right: Church of the Nativity, Bethlehem.

Below: Hills of Egypt's Sinai Desert lead down to the blue waters of the Red Sea.

his faith. The Lord intervened to save Isaac and provided a ram to be sacrificed instead. Here Abraham experienced God's intervening presence and in recognition of this he named the place 'The Lord will provide.' (See Genesis 22.)

Red Sea: this is the name given in the Bible to an area of water that the Israelites had to cross when they fled Egypt. It is difficult to locate precisely – it could be the marshy area north of the Gulf of Suez called 'the Sea of Reeds' – although it is clearly associated with the Gulf of Suez region. Throughout the Bible the Israelites celebrate the fact that their God delivered them miraculously from the pursuing Egyptian armies at this place. (Exodus 13 – 14:31.)

Susa: this was the capital city of the Persian empire during the reign of Xerxes. The Jewish festival of Purim celebrates the miraculous delivery of the Jews of the Persian empire from an annihilation plot (see chapter 4, **Esther**). (See Esther 9.)

Tower of Babel: Babel means 'gate of God', and the Tower of Babel was intended to reach to heaven. God intervened to scatter the people who were building it and confuse their languages so that they could not understand one another. It is most likely that the sin that comes to judgment here is human pride, trying to usurp God. The name 'Babel' is obviously connected to Babylon, although it is uncertain whether the geographical places are one and the same (see Genesis 11).

Places in Jesus' life

The map (right) shows where Jesus' life events took place. The places are divided into five sections by association with (i) his life from birth to baptism (orange); (ii) his ministry in Galilee (blue); (iii) his journey from Galilee to Jerusalem (green); (iv) his final week (red – see map p. 147); (v) his resurrection appearances (purple).

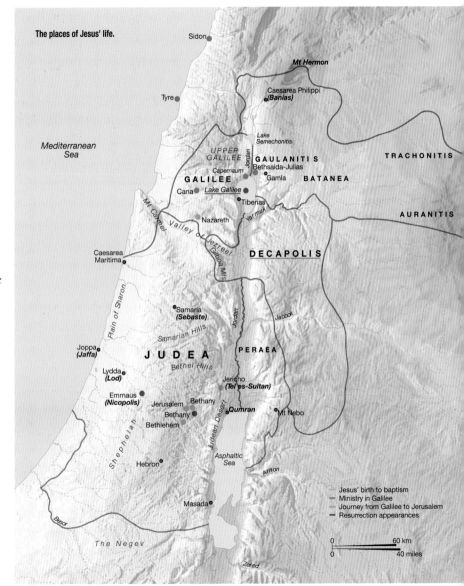

The places of Jesus' life.

Sidon

Mt Hermon

Tyre

Caesarea Philippi
(Banias)

Mediterranean Sea

Lake Semechonitis

UPPER GALILEE
Jordan
GAULANITIS
Capernaum
Bethsaida-Julias
TRACHONITIS
GALILEE
Gamla
BATANEA
Cana
Lake Galilee
Tiberias
AURANITIS
Nazareth
Yarmuk

Mt Carmel

Valley of Jezreel / Gilboa Mts

DECAPOLIS

Caesarea Maritima

Plain of Sharon

Samaria
(Sebaste)

Jordan

Jabbok

Samarian Hills

Joppa
(Jaffa)

PERAEA

JUDEA
Bethel Hills

Lydda
(Lod)

Jericho
(Tel es-Sultan)

Emmaus
(Nicopolis)

Jerusalem
Bethany

Bethany

Judean Desert

Qumran

Mt Nebo

Bethlehem

Shephelah

Hebron

Asphaltic Sea

Arnon

Besor

Masada

Jesus' birth to baptism
Ministry in Galilee
Journey from Galilee to Jerusalem
Resurrection appearances

The Negev

0   60 km
0   40 miles

Zered

(i) From birth to baptism

Bethlehem: the small town, south of Jerusalem, where Jesus was born (see Matthew 2:1; Luke 2:1–7).

Egypt: Jesus and his family escaped to Egypt shortly after Jesus' birth and stayed there until Herod died (see Matthew 2:13–18).

Nazareth: the small village set in the Galilean hills where Jesus grew up (see Matthew 2:19–23).

Jerusalem: as a child Jesus went to Jerusalem with his parents. He was left behind there on one occasion, and his parents had to travel back to find him. He was found in the city's Temple precincts (see Luke 2:41–52; John 2:12–25).

River Jordan: this was the place where Jesus was baptized by John the Baptist before he began his public ministry (see Matthew 3:13–17; Mark 1:9–11; Luke 3:21–22; John 1:31–34).

(ii) Ministry in Galilee

Cana: Cana was a small village in Galilee, not far from Jesus' home town of Nazareth. There Jesus performed his first miracle, turning water into wine at a wedding feast. He also met an official whose son was ill, and healed him, even though the boy was some distance away in Capernaum (see John 2:1–11; 4:43–54).

Sychar: Sychar was in Samaria, and there Jesus met and spoke with a Samaritan

The ruins of a synagogue at the ancient city of Capernaum.

woman at Jacob's well (John 4:4–26).

Capernaum: situated on the shore of the Sea of Galilee, this town was the focus for much of Jesus' teaching and early ministry. Matthew calls Capernaum Jesus' 'own town', suggesting that Jesus considered it to be his base. It was an important town for his ministry, although its people did not always accept his teaching, and it was the home town of many of his disciples. Jesus performed healing miracles there and taught in the synagogue (see Matthew 9:1; Mark 1:16–21, 29; 2:13–14; 9:1–9; John 6:59).

Caesarea Philippi: this was a large city on the slopes of Mount Hermon, where Peter made his famous declaration that he believed Jesus was the messiah (see Matthew 16:13–20; Mark 8:27).

Bethsaida: on the shore of the Sea of Galilee, Bethsaida was the home town of Philip, Andrew and Peter. It was probably the nearest town to where the feeding of the 5,000 and Jesus' walking on water took place (see John 12:21).

(iii) Journey from Galilee to Jerusalem

Bethany: Bethany was a small village on the outskirts of Jerusalem, near the Mount of Olives, where Lazarus and his sisters Mary and Martha lived. Jesus often stayed there and he performed the miracle of raising Lazarus from the dead in Bethany. It was here that Mary anointed Jesus with oil (see John 11:1–44; John 12: 1–11).

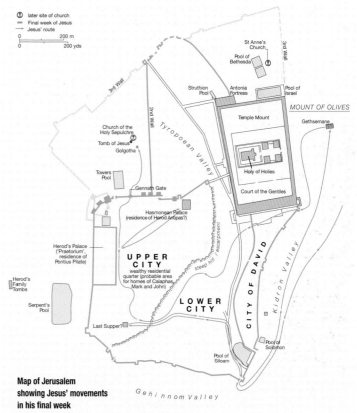

later site of church
Final week of Jesus
Jesus' route

0   200 m
0   200 yds

3rd Wall

St Anne's
Church

Pool of
Bethesda

3rd Wall

2nd Wall

Struthion
Pool

Antonia
Fortress

Pool of
Israel

Tyropoean Valley

MOUNT OF OLIVES

Church of the
Holy Sepulchre

Temple Mount

Gethsemane

Tomb of Jesus
Golgotha

Holy of Holies

Towers
Pool

Court of the Gentiles

Gennath Gate

Hasmonean Palace
(residence of Herod Antipas?)

steep hill escarpment

Herod's Palace
('Praetorium',
residence of
Pontius Pilate)

**UPPER
CITY**
wealthy residential
quarter (probable area
for homes of Caiaphas,
Mark and John)

CITY OF DAVID

Kidron Valley

Herod's
Family
Tombs

**LOWER
CITY**

Serpent's
Pool

Last Supper?

Pool of
Solomon

Pool of
Siloam

**Map of Jerusalem
showing Jesus' movements
in his final week**

Gehinnom Valley

Mount Hermon: this impressive mountain,
the highest in Palestine, was always
considered a sacred location and it was
possibly the location for the transfiguration
of Jesus (see Matthew 17:1–9; Mark 9:2, 9;
Luke 9:28).

Siloam: when Jesus healed a man who had
been born blind he told the man to go and
wash in the pool of Siloam in Jerusalem. It
was part of the water supply structures built
by King Hezekiah to supply the city (see
John 9:1–41).

(iv) Final week in Jerusalem
Kidron brook: the Kidron brook was

formed by water running down a valley in
the eastern regions of Jerusalem. Jesus and
his disciples crossed this valley on their way
to the Garden of Gethsemane (John 18:1).

Bethphage: Bethphage was a village near
Jerusalem which is mentioned in the
accounts of Jesus' entry into Jerusalem. It

Top left: View of the Old
City of Jerusalem and
the Mount of Olives,
Jerusalem.

The spread of the gospel in Acts

The impetus for the spread of the gospel began with the commission at the start of Acts: 'You shall be my witnesses in Jerusalem and in Judea and Samaria and to the ends of the earth' (Acts 1:8). In the accounts of Acts, Christianity spread out across the Roman empire from Jerusalem to Rome. The first seven chapters focus on the Christian community based in Jerusalem, and then, in chapters 8–12, the new faith spreads in Judea and Samaria. Paul and Barnabas are then sent out from Antioch to Cyprus, Pisidian Antioch, Iconium and Lystra (12:25 – 15:40), before Paul embarks on further missionary journeys in Asia Minor and Greece (chapters 16–20). The remaining chapters follow Paul back to Jerusalem and then onwards to Rome (chapters 21–28).

In this detail from the early 14th-century Maesta altarpiece by Duccio di Buoninsegna, Jesus appears to two disciples on the road to Emmaus.

was there that the disciples found the donkey for Jesus to ride in the events commemorated on Palm Sunday (see Matthew 21:1; Mark 11:1; Luke 19:29).

Golgotha: the name Golgotha means 'the place of the skull'; the Latin version of the name is **Calvary**. This was the site of the crucifixion of Jesus. The exact location is not clear, but it would have been outside Jerusalem's city wall. There was a garden close by to which Jesus' body was taken after he died, to be buried in a tomb belonging to Joseph of Arimathea (see Matthew 27:33; Mark 15:22; John 19:17).

(v) Resurrection appearances

Jesus appeared to his disciples after his death at the tomb near Golgotha; in a room, probably in Jerusalem; on the shore of the Sea of Galilee; on the road to Emmaus and

probably on the Mount of Olives. Jesus ascended into heaven before his disciples at a location near Bethany (Matthew 28; Mark 16; Luke 24; John 20–21; Acts 1).

Places associated with journeys

Cities

Antioch: this was the third largest city in the Roman empire and Paul's base, from which he set out on his missionary journeys. It was in Antioch that followers of Jesus were first called 'Christians' (Acts 11:26; 13:1ff; 15:36ff; 18:23ff.).

Islands

Crete, Cyprus, Malta, Rhodes: these were important Mediterranean islands visited by Paul on his great missionary journeys. Paul's companion Barnabas came from Cyprus. Paul himself was shipwrecked off the coast of Malta. Rhodes was a Greek island where Paul's ship made a stop on his last journey to Jerusalem (Acts 13:5–13; 21:1; 27:8; 28:1–10).

Rivers

Jordan: crossing the River Jordan was an important milestone in the Israelite tribes' journey to the Promised Land. It was crossed at a number of fords along its 200-mile (322 km) course, which were always key military points (Joshua 3).

Roads

To Damascus: Saul saw a vision of Jesus on the road to Damascus. Dramatic conversions to the Christian faith today are sometimes called 'Damascus road experiences'(Acts 9:1–31).

To Emmaus: Jesus appeared to two men walking on the road from Jerusalem to the village of Emmaus following his resurrection. Jesus talked with them about the events that had happened surrounding his crucifixion. Once they realized that they had spoken with the risen Christ, they made their way to Jerusalem to tell the disciples (Luke 24:13–35).

To Jericho: the road from Jerusalem to Jericho is the location for one of Jesus' most well-known parables, the parable of the Good Samaritan (Matthew 22:34–40; Mark 12:28–31; Luke 10:25–37).

King's highway: this was a very important trade route that ran along the eastern boundary of Palestine from Damascus to the Gulf of Aqabah. It also connected with Egyptian trade routes and as such brought commercial opportunities as well as foreign religious influences to the territories through which it ran (Numbers 20:17–21; 21:22; Deuteronomy 2:27).

Wilderness

Sinai desert: the people of Israel wandered in the desert region of the Sinai peninsula under Moses' leadership for forty years, having left Egypt and heading towards Canaan. It was the place where their faith was tested but where God provided for them (Deuteronomy 2:1 – 3:11).

Places of sin

Gehenna: in Old Testament times this valley, south of Jerusalem, was the site of the pagan worship of Molech. The rites included children being burnt as sacrifices. By the time the New Testament was written the term 'gehenna', which means 'fiery hell', was used to mean the place of fiery punishment after death for those who were wicked and unrepentant (2 Kings 23:10; 2 Chronicles 28:3; Jeremiah 7:31; Psalms 18:8; 50:3; Matthew 5:22; 10:33; James 3:6).

Nineveh: this was the capital city of the Assyrian empire, an empire that the Israelites always feared

Lot's wife looks backwards (Genesis 19) in the 13th-century Poor Man's Bible window, panel in Canterbury Cathedral, UK.

The Karnak Temple Complex's relief sculpture of slaves in the precinct of Amun-Re, the Egyptian god.

Places of exile and captivity

Babylon: the capital city of the Babylonian empire represented captivity to the people of Israel following their exile there under King Nebuchadnezzar. (See chapter 4, **Fall of Babylon**.)

Egypt: God's people found themselves slaves in the land of Egypt prior to Moses' leading them away from Pharaoh's tyranny. Throughout their history the Israelites feared the strength and enmity of Egypt. (See Exodus 1–12; Isaiah 20.) (See chapter 4, **Exodus**.)

Patmos: this was a Greek island to which the Roman authorities sometimes banished political prisoners. John was exiled here when he wrote the book of Revelation (see Revelation 1:9).

because of its power. When Jonah was sent to this wicked city by God he decided to run away. Other prophets, including Nahum and Zephaniah, also confronted its wickedness but foresaw the time when Nineveh would fall to the Babylonians. (See chapter 4, books of **Jonah, Nahum** and **Zephaniah**.)

Rome: the capital of the Roman empire becomes, under the name of Babylon, a symbol of power turned into rebellion against God in the book of Revelation. (See references to Babylon in Revelation 17:1 – 19:5.) (See chapter 5, **Revelation**; chapter 1, **Apocalyptic literature**.)

Sodom and Gomorrah: during the time of Abraham these two cities were known for their wickedness and were destroyed by fire. They have become proverbial as places of sin and rebellion (Genesis 18:16 – 19:29).

Places of hope

Cities of refuge: these six cities were scattered throughout the Promised Land and were designated as places of refuge from punishment for people who had been found guilty of accidentally killing someone (see Numbers 35:6–7; Deuteronomy 4:41–43; Joshua 20:7).

Jerusalem: the royal city of David and his son Solomon, also referred to in the Bible as Zion, Moriah and Salem. The Psalms in particular celebrate Jerusalem as Zion, the city that has God's special favour and protection. During New Testament times Jerusalem was under Roman rule, although the Temple remained in Jewish hands.(See chapters 4 and 5, Overviews of the Old Testament and New Testament.)

Mount Ararat: this mountain in Armenia was a place associated with hope for Noah and his family because it was the first dry ground to appear when the flood waters receded and was where the Ark came to rest (see Genesis 8:4).

New Jerusalem: the book of Revelation ends with a vision of a renewed Jerusalem. This represents the hope for God's people that the injustices of the world will come to an end and God will finally establish his rule on earth as he dwells with his people (see Revelation 21).

Promised Land: the land of Canaan that the Israelite tribes entered and conquered was always called the Promised Land, in recognition that it meant the fulfilment of the promise made to Abraham that God's people would be given a land to possess (see Genesis 15; Deuteronomy 4; Joshua 1ff).

Further reading suggestions

Bimson, John J. (consulting editor), *Illustrated Encyclopedia of Bible Places*, Leicester, InterVartisty Press, 1995.

Mount Ararat, Armenia.

The Bible and Christian Belief

The heart of biblical faith

This chapter examines two different ways of considering the essential ingredients of biblical faith. It looks at the beliefs expressed within the Bible and identifies where those beliefs are found in the Christian church today.

St Andrew's Church, Good Easter, UK.

Christians believe that the practices of the church express the beliefs about God and the world that are presented in the Bible. These beliefs are celebrated in the church's worship. When Christians first gathered together, they declared the faith they had come to share. Going back further, these Christian beliefs themselves had their foundations in the pages of the Old Testament, which also contains words that were, and are, frequently repeated by Jewish people in their worship as

statements of faith. So it is appropriate to look at biblical faith through the lens of worship: what does the worship life of the church tell us about the nature and content of biblical faith?

Obviously this approach itself emphasizes

the belief that biblical faith finds its meaning and purpose in worship. Biblical faith is not authentic if it is not worked out in practical responses in the worship life of its adherents. That is why theology can never be a purely academic discipline: it demands an integrated environment where learning, living, praying and practising the faith each have their place. Christians since the birth of the church have always sought to express their belief first in statements of faith (creeds or credal statements)

Council of Nicaea, as depicted in an 18th-century icon by the Novogrod School.

attention to the interconnectedness of belief and worship.

Biblical faith and church creeds

Many Christian people would automatically think about the church's creeds if they were asked to outline the key doctrines of their faith. There are various different creeds used across the range of Christian churches that exist today, but all act in some way or other as summaries of the Christian belief system. In addition, some Christian groups and associations have statements of faith which serve a similar purpose, but in this chapter we will focus on the creeds that are used within the context of Christian worship, for the reasons explained.

Creeds are not meant to be totally comprehensive and detailed theological expositions, but they are intended to express the core beliefs that unify the Christian church. Creeds also guard the church against heretical extremes. They preserve the agreed words that have come into being as the result of much lengthy debate, controversy and struggle. Creeds can be used in either corporate or private worship and can serve to teach, reaffirm and encourage faith. In this sense they really 'shape' the Christian church, forming the basis of its practices and activities.

Here are two creeds that have been used by the church over the centuries.

The first is called the **Apostles' Creed** and, in its earliest form, dates within fifty years of the last New Testament writings.

and secondly through regular services of worship (liturgy). These two expressions of faith are useful frameworks for looking at Christian belief while also drawing

The title respects the fact that this credal statement was understood at an early time to be a summary of the apostles' teaching. It was probably used as a form of words to be repeated by new converts when they were baptized and became members of the early Christian communities. Notice the various paragraphs that express different key themes of Christian belief:

I believe in God, the Father Almighty,
the Creator of heaven and earth,
and in Jesus Christ, His only Son, our
Lord:

Who was conceived of the Holy Spirit,
born of the Virgin Mary,
suffered under Pontius Pilate,
was crucified, died, and was buried.

He descended into hell.

The third day He arose again from the
dead.

He ascended into heaven
and sits at the right hand of God the
Father Almighty,
whence He shall come to judge the living
and the dead.

I believe in the Holy Spirit, the holy catholic
church,
the communion of saints,
the forgiveness of sins,
the resurrection of the body,
and life everlasting.

Amen.

Notice that the main attention seems to be focused on Jesus and the key events of his lifetime.

A later creed, the **Nicene Creed**, also popular in the church today, had its origins in the fourth century and while maintaining the same basic structure, it is different in its details as it unpacks some of the earlier creed's statements.

I believe in one God, the Father Almighty,
Maker of heaven and earth, and of all
things visible and invisible.

And in one Lord Jesus Christ, the only
begotten Son of God, begotten of the Father
before all worlds; God of God, Light of
Light, very God of very God; begotten,
not made, being of one substance with the
Father, by whom all things were made.

Who, for us men and for our salvation,
came down from heaven, and was
incarnate by the Holy Spirit of the virgin
Mary, and was made man; and was
crucified also for us under Pontius Pilate;
He suffered and was buried; and the
third day He rose again, according to the
Scriptures; and ascended into heaven, and
sits on the right hand of the Father; and He
shall come again, with glory, to judge the
quick and the dead; whose kingdom shall
have no end.

And I believe in the Holy Ghost/Spirit, the
Lord and Giver of Life; who proceeds from
the Father and the Son; who with the Father
and the Son together is worshipped and
glorified; who spoke by the prophets.

Unpacking Bible beliefs: Who is God? What is God like?

The Bible uses many names for God. These are sometimes used interchangeably but they have more specific meanings and emphases too. They are theologically loaded names which reflect people's experience and understanding of God. They include:

- **God**: the divine being and creator of the world;
- **Lord**: the one who is sovereign;
- **Lord (Yahweh)**: the one who comes to his people in covenant; the eternal, active, self-sustaining, self-revealing, all present, holy and unique personal God;
- **compound names**: the Lord God; God Most High; Lord of hosts (Lord Almighty); the Lord is peace (Judges 6:24); the Lord provides (Genesis 22:8); the Lord is my banner (Exodus 17:15); the Lord our righteousness (Jeremiah 23:6); the Lord is there (Ezekiel 48:35); the God who sees me (Genesis 16:13);
- **Images**: shepherd (Psalm 23), rock (Psalm 78:35), fortress (Psalm 18:2), refuge (Psalm 91:2), shield (Deuteronomy 33:29).

Another way of understanding the nature of God is to think about the characteristics of God that are unique. Christians believe the Bible teaches that God is:

- omnipotent: all-powerful;
- omniscient: all-knowing;
- omnipresent: present everywhere;
- eternal: he was, is and always will be;
- morally perfect: holy;
- immutable: he does not change;
- incomprehensible: humanity cannot comprehend him.

And I believe in one holy catholic and apostolic church. I acknowledge one baptism for the remission of sins; and I look for the resurrection of the dead, and the life of the world to come.

Amen.

So it is quite clear from just a brief look at these creeds that Christian belief includes statements about:

- God the Father;
- God the Son (Jesus);
- God the Holy Spirit;
- the universal church;
- salvation (forgiveness of sins; eternal life).

These key elements of faith also feature within the Bible. Take, for example, the following verses about God the Father:

Hear, O Israel: the Lord our God, the Lord is one. Love the Lord your God with all your heart and with all your soul and with all your strength.
DEUTERONOMY 6:4–5

The Lord, the Lord, the compassionate and gracious God, slow to anger, abounding in love and faithfulness, maintaining love to thousands, and forgiving wickedness, rebellion and sin.
EXODUS 34:6–7

The Lord is the everlasting God, the Creator of the ends of the earth.
ISAIAH 40:28

Unpacking Bible beliefs:
Who is Jesus? What is Jesus like?

Who is Jesus? The Gospel writers tell us that even during Jesus' lifetime this question was discussed. The Gospel writers answer the question in three ways:

1. They tell us what the disciples (and other people) thought.
2. They tell us what Jesus himself said.
3. They give us clues about their own understanding in the design of their Gospels, looking back at the events of Jesus' lifetime that they had witnessed. Their opinions about Jesus are supplemented by those of other New Testament writers. Together they draw on the Old Testament and claim that the ancient Jewish texts also tell us important things about Jesus.

Here are some of the comments made by Jesus' disciples and others who met him:

- Two blind men said: 'Lord, Son of David, have mercy on us' (Matthew 20:30).
- John the Baptist said: 'Look the Lamb of God, who takes away the sin of the world' (John 1:29).
- On Jesus' cross the words were written: 'Jesus, the King of the Jews' (Matthew 27:37).
- A Roman centurion said, 'Surely he was the Son of God' (Matthew 27:54).

Other titles used to address Jesus or speak about him include: Rabbi (John 1:38); Immanuel ('God with us') (Matthew 1:23); Jesus of Nazareth (John 1:45); rising sun (Luke 1:78).

Here are some of the things that Jesus said about himself:

- 'I am the bread of life' (John 6:35).
- 'I am the light of the world' (John 8:12).
- 'Before Abraham was born, I am' (John 8:58).
- 'I am the good shepherd' (John 10:11).
- 'I am the resurrection and the life' (John 11:25).
- 'I am the way, the truth and the life' (John 14:6).
- 'I am the true vine' (John 15:1).

Each Gospel writer has a different emphasis when it comes to presenting Jesus to his readers. For example, we could say that:

- *Matthew* portrays Jesus primarily as rabbi: the teacher of the Jews;
- *Mark* portrays Jesus primarily as the suffering messiah;
- *Luke* portrays Jesus primarily as the saviour of the world;
- *John* portrays Jesus primarily as the divine Son and Word of God.

In other New Testament books we find some additional titles and descriptions applied to Jesus:

- 'Prince and Saviour' (Acts 5:31);
- 'Righteous One' (Acts 7:52);
- 'Passover lamb' (1 Corinthians 5:7);
- 'The image of the invisible God, the firstborn over all creation' (Colossians 1:15);
- 'Head of the Church' (Colossians 1:18);
- 'One mediator between God and humanity, the man Christ Jesus, who gave himself as a ransom for all people' (1 Timothy 2:5–6);
- 'Saviour' (Titus 1:4);
- 'High Priest' (Hebrews 3:1);
- 'The author and perfecter of our salvation' (Hebrews 12:2);
- 'Lion of Judah' (Revelation 5:5);
- 'Alpha and Omega' (Revelation 22:13);
- 'Bright morning star'; 'Root and offspring of David' (Revelation 22:16).

Close-up view of the crucifix at St George's Basilica, Malta.

The Trinity in the Bible

Christian people believe the Bible teaches that there are three distinct persons who make up the Godhead: the Father, the Son and the Holy Spirit. Bible verses which mention all three persons are few, but they are important ones in the Christian tradition:

'Therefore go and make disciples of all nations, baptising them in the name of the Father, Son and Holy Spirit...'

MATTHEW 28:19

'May the grace of the Lord Jesus Christ, and the love of God and the fellowship of the Holy Spirit be with you all.'

2 CORINTHIANS 13:14

But there are other verses which explain the work and presence of God by referring to the persons of the Trinity by name. Here are a few examples:

'But when the kindness and love of God our Saviour appeared, he saved us, not because of righteous things we had done, but because of his mercy. He saved us through the washing of rebirth and renewal by the Holy Spirit, whom he poured out on us generously, through Jesus Christ our Saviour...'

TITUS 3:4–6

'To God's elect... who have been chosen according to the foreknowledge of God the Father, through the sanctifying work of the Spirit, for obedience to Jesus Christ and sprinkling by his blood.'

1 PETER 1:1–2

(See also 2 Corinthians 1:21–22; Ephesians 2:20–22; 2 Thessalonians 2:13–14.)

What we have, then, in the New Testament is an understanding of God and his work which requires an understanding of God as Trinity. It is assumed that God is both set apart from the world and present in the world in his work of creation and salvation. The same assumption appears in the Old Testament through the use of the ideas of the Spirit, wisdom and Word of God.

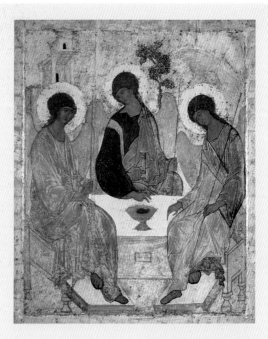

Icon of *The Holy Trinity* by Andrei Rublev, (1370–1430).

The Lord your God is with you, he is mighty to save.

ZEPHANIAH 3:17

All the sentiments in these verses are repeated over and over again in the Bible, and they reaffirm the importance of believing certain things about God the Father.

In the New Testament we have some early examples of creed-like statements, possibly already in use in early Christian communities. The focus is upon Jesus:

Your attitude should be the same as that of Christ Jesus: Who being in very nature God, did not consider equality with God something to be grasped, but made himself nothing, taking the very nature of a servant, being made in human likeness. And being found in appearance as a man, he humbled himself and became obedient to death – even death on a cross! Therefore God exalted him to the highest place and gave him the name that is above every name, that at the name of Jesus every knee should bow and every tongue confess that Jesus Christ is Lord to the glory of God the Father.

PHILIPPIANS 2:5–11

Beyond all question, the mystery of godliness is great: He appeared in a body, was vindicated by the Spirit, was seen by angels, was preached among the nations, was believed on in the world, was taken up in glory.

1 TIMOTHY 3:16

Unpacking Bible beliefs: Who is the Holy Spirit? What is the Holy Spirit like?

The Bible asserts the following things about the Holy Spirit:
- He is active in creation (Genesis 1:2).
- He is equal with the Father and the Son, and is sent out into the world by the Father and the Son (Matthew 28:19; John 15:26).
- He is called 'the Counsellor' (John 16:5); 'the Spirit of truth' (John 16:13); 'the Lord' (2 Corinthians 3:17).
- The church received the Holy Spirit on the day of Pentecost and he inspired their worship and mission (Acts 2).
- His work includes: guiding people in the truth (John 16:13); 'convicting the world of sin, righteousness and judgment' (John 16:8); acting as a seal of ownership on believers (Ephesians 1:13); giving assurance of faith (Ephesians 4:16); giving victory to God's people (Judges 3:10); giving life (Ezekiel 37:14); teaching (1 Corinthians 2:13); producing fruit in the life of the believer (including love, joy, peace, patience, kindness, goodness, faithfulness, gentleness and self-control) (Galatians 5:22); restraining God's people (Acts 16:6–7).
- He is described as like a dove (Matthew 3:16); wind or breath (Acts 2:2); fire (Acts 2:4; 1 Thessalonians 5:19); living water (John 7:38–39).

Creeds and theology

Here is a table presenting the Nicene Creed alongside a theological textbook that discusses the development and content of Christian belief over the centuries. This example illustrates how the church's creeds have provided a framework for the discussion of Christian belief.

Creed	Chapter headings from a standard Christian theology book[1]
I believe in one God, the Father Almighty, Maker of heaven and earth, and of all things visible and invisible.	The Doctrine of God
And in one Lord Jesus Christ, the only-begotten Son of God, begotten of the Father before all worlds; God of God, Light of Light, very God of very God; begotten, not made, being of one substance with the Father, by whom all things were made.	The Doctrine of the Trinity
Who, for us men and for our salvation, came down from heaven, and was incarnate by the Holy Spirit of the virgin Mary, and was made man;	The Doctrine of the Person of Christ
and was crucified also for us under Pontius Pilate; He suffered and was buried; and the third day He rose again, according to the Scriptures; and ascended into heaven, and sits on the right hand of the Father; and He shall come again, with glory, to judge the quick and the dead; whose kingdom shall have no end.	The Doctrine of Salvation in Christ
And I believe in the Holy Ghost, the Lord and Giver of Life; who proceeds from the Father and the Son; who with the Father and the Son together is worshipped and glorified; who spoke by the prophets.	The Holy Spirit[2]
And I believe in one holy catholic and apostolic church.	The Doctrine of the Church
I acknowledge one baptism for the remission of sins;	The Doctrine of the Sacraments
and I look for the resurrection of the dead, and the life of the world to come. Amen.	Last Things: The Christian Hope

Yet for us there is but one God, the Father, from whom all things came and for whom we live; and there is but one Lord, Jesus Christ, through whom all things came and through whom we live.

1 CORINTHIANS 8:6

But notice two things here:
(i) the statement of faith from 1 Timothy already says something about the role of the Holy Spirit in relation to the life of Jesus. We also find in the New Testament a variety of statements about the Holy Spirit that express emerging belief about the Spirit's person and work:

To God's elect... who have been chosen according to the foreknowledge of God the Father, through the sanctifying work of the Spirit, for obedience to Jesus Christ and sprinkling by his blood...

1 PETER 1:1–2

And if the Spirit of him who raised Jesus from the dead is living in you, he who raised Christ from the dead will also give life to your mortal bodies through his Spirit, who lives in you.

ROMANS 8:11

(ii) the statement of faith in 1 Corinthians 8:6 already hints at a discussion about the relationship of the Father to the Son and in particular emphasizes the Son's role and activity in creation. A similar emphasis is found in other New Testament verses:

The Son is the radiance of God's glory and the exact representation of his being,

sustaining all things by his powerful word. After he had provided purification for sins, he sat down at the right hand of the Majesty in heaven.

HEBREWS 1:3

He is the image of the invisible God, the firstborn over all creation. For by him all things were created: things in heaven and on earth... All things were created by him and for him. He is before all things, and in him all things hold together. And he is the head of the body, the church...

COLOSSIANS 1:15–20

In the beginning was the Word, and the Word was with God and the Word was God.'

JOHN 1:1

While summaries of these beliefs entered the creeds, discussions about the meaning and implications of such verses continued to occupy Christian theologians over the centuries.

In the book of Revelation we find further statements about salvation, the universal kingdom of God and the age to come. Many of these are clearly worship declarations and consequently it is hardly surprising that their sentiments too infiltrated the Christian creeds:

The kingdom of the world has become the kingdom of our Lord and of his Christ, and he will reign for ever and ever.

REVELATION 11:17

*We give thanks to you, Lord, God
Almighty, the One who is and who was,
because you have taken your great power
and have begun to reign.*
REVELATION 11:17

*Now have come the salvation and the
power and the kingdom of our God, and the
authority of his Christ.*
REVELATION 12:10

*Look, he is coming with the clouds, and
every eye will see him, even those who
pierced him; and all the peoples of the earth
will mourn because of him. So shall it be!
Amen.*
REVELATION 1:7

It is clear that within the Bible there are
early examples of belief statements that in
turn became incorporated into Christian
creeds used in the early church as well
as in the church today. Many theological
textbooks today take their structure
from these creeds, attempting to explore
the intricacies of belief that the creeds
themselves can only summarize.

Biblical faith and the Christian calendar

Over the centuries, another approach to
theological discussion has emerged that
relies on a different element of Christian
worship – the regular events of the
Christian calendar or, to use slightly more
technical language, the liturgical structure
of the church year.[3] It is hardly surprising
that the calendar of the church reflects its

major beliefs, but the regular divisions
of the Christian calendar also allow
statements of faith to find their context in
the structures that the church has adopted
for worship. Again, this emphasizes that
theology and belief find their *raison
d'être* when worked out in the response of
worship and discipleship.

One of the main advantages of adhering
to regular events in the Christian calendar
is that in its annual programme the church
bears witness to the gospel story. The
calendar itself serves as an invitation to
embark on a journey of faith, a process of
discovery, in order to encounter the main
episodes of the biblical story. This journey
has transforming qualities because when
Christians participate in it, they follow the
same path that Jesus walked and countless
generations of his followers have walked
ever since, and they can allow themselves to
be shaped by it.

The Christian church's calendar today is
structured around the seven seasons of the
Christian year.[4] Christian people in many
different churches and throughout the
world use this calendar, or a similar one, to
order their private and corporate devotions.
These seven seasons can be identified as set
out in the table above, and linked with the
major theological themes indicated.

It is certainly true that in these
theological statements we have a
comprehensive summary of the main
components of Christian belief. In fact if
you compare this summary with the content
of one of the earliest recorded Christian
sermons you can see that they both share a

Christian season	Theological theme
1. The season of Advent	God is the one who comes.
2. The season of Christmas	God is the one who takes our humanity.
3. The season of Epiphany	God is the one who is revealed.
4. The season of Lent	God is the one who journeys to the cross.
5. The season of Easter	God is the one who lives and reigns.
6. The season of Pentecost	God is the one who indwells and transforms.
7. The season of the kingdom	God is the one who invites us into communion.

common set of theological statements:

Then Peter stood up with the Eleven, raised his voice and addressed the crowd: 'Fellow Jews and all of you who live in Jerusalem, let me explain this to you; listen carefully to what I say. These men are not drunk, as you suppose. It's only nine in the morning! No, this is what was spoken by the prophet Joel:

"In the last days, God says,
I will pour out my Spirit on all people.
Your sons and daughters will prophesy,
your young men will see visions,
your old men will dream dreams.
Even on my servants, both men and women,
I will pour out my Spirit in those days,
and they will prophesy.
I will show wonders in the heaven above
and signs on the earth below,
blood and fire and billows of smoke.
The sun will be turned to darkness
and the moon to blood
before the coming of the great and glorious
day of the Lord.
And everyone who calls
on the name of the Lord will be saved."

'Men of Israel, listen to this: Jesus of Nazareth was a man accredited by God to you by miracles, wonders and signs, which God did among you through him, as you yourselves know. This man was handed over to you by God's set purpose and foreknowledge; and you, with the help of wicked men, put him to death by nailing him to the cross. But God raised him from the dead, freeing him from the agony of death, because it was impossible for death to keep its hold on him. David said about him:

'"I saw the Lord always before me.
Because he is at my right hand,
I will not be shaken.

What does the Bible say about faith and belief?

So what does the Bible itself say about faith and belief? We can turn to the book of the Psalms and see how belief and faith lead to prayers of devotion, honesty and worship. Psalms 42–43 (possibly originally one psalm) are a good example of how, in the Bible, belief is not about intellect and knowledge but about a personal response to God which finds expression in prayer and worship and a life lived for God.

Other verses speak of the nature of faith:

'Now faith is being sure of what we hope for and certain of what we do not see.'

HEBREWS 11:1–2

These verses are followed by a list of people from the Old Testament who lived their lives 'by faith'. What is clear is that faith and belief had an impact on the life choices of these people. Paul says that faith is in fact the basis and the means of living of every aspect of his life:

'The life I live in the body, I live by faith in the Son of God, who loved me and gave himself for me.'

GALATIANS 2:20

James says that actions are the mark of true faith:

'What good is it, my brothers, if a man claims to have faith but has no deeds? Can such faith save him? ... faith by itself, if it is not accompanied by action, is dead.'

JAMES 2:14–17

In the Bible life and faith, beliefs about God and the response to God in worship, can never be separated.

Therefore my heart is glad and my tongue rejoices;
my body also will live in hope,
because you will not abandon me to the grave,
nor will you let your Holy One see decay.
You have made known to me the paths of life;
you will fill me with joy in your presence.'

'Brothers, I can tell you confidently that the patriarch David died and was buried, and his tomb is here to this day. But he was a prophet and knew that God had promised him on oath that he would place one of his descendants on his throne. Seeing what was ahead, he spoke of the resurrection of the Christ, that he was not abandoned to the grave, nor did his body see decay. God has raised this Jesus to life, and we are all witnesses of the fact. Exalted to the right hand of God, he has received from the Father the promised Holy Spirit and has poured out what you now see and hear. For David did not ascend to heaven, and yet he said,

'"The Lord said to my Lord:
'Sit at my right hand
until I make your enemies
a footstool for your feet.'"

'Therefore let all Israel be assured of this: God has made this Jesus, whom you crucified, both Lord and Christ.'

When the people heard this, they were cut to the heart and said to Peter and the other apostles, 'Brothers, what shall we do?'

Peter replied, 'Repent and be baptised,

every one of you, in the name of Jesus Christ for the forgiveness of your sins. And you will receive the gift of the Holy Spirit. The promise is for you and your children and for all who are far off – for all whom the Lord our God will call.'

With many other words he warned them; and he pleaded with them, 'Save yourselves from this corrupt generation.' Those who accepted his message were baptized, and about three thousand were added to their number that day.

ACTS 2:14–41

It is clear that this sermon, like the structure of the Christian calendar, takes its lead from the biblical story itself and connects the theology that emerges from that story to the worship and life responses of Christians. In this way the method or structure of theological reflection and discussion actually supports their goal, and indeed the purpose of the Bible. The Bible itself (as we have already considered in chapter 1) takes Christians on a journey of faith as they witness God's emerging faith in his people. By using the structure of the Christian year to examine theological belief we are reminded too of the Christian faith's historical roots, because it is grounded in beliefs about Jesus. We reflect that, as the creeds themselves conclude, Christians have a keen sense of the church as universal and eternal. The church reaches back to the first believers in Jesus and reaches forward to the coming kingdom. In the meantime, in its corporate worship (whether by

creeds, calendar, hymns, prayers, words or deeds) it declares its core beliefs.

Further reading suggestions

Doug Connelly and Martin Manser, *Christianity for Blockheads: A User-Friendly Look at What Christians Believe*, Grand Rapids, Zondervan, 2009

J. Colwell, *Rhythm of Doctrine*, Colorado Springs: Paternoster, 2007.

Michael Lloyd, *Café Theology*, Alpha International, 2005.

Martin H. Manser (ed), *Collins Bible Companion*, London: HarperCollins, 2009

Alister McGrath, *Christian Theology: An Introduction*, Oxford: Blackwell, 1994; and *New Dictionary of Biblical Theology*, Leicester: IVP, 2000.

10

Reading and Using the Bible Today

How to read the Bible

This final chapter considers how the Bible should be read. Christians believe that reading the Bible is an essential part of their individual devotional life as well as the corporate life they share with other Christians. Most Christians believe it is good to read their Bibles regularly, although sometimes they find it difficult to do this.

'What is the Bible but a letter of God Almighty addressed to his creatures, in which we hear the voice of God and behold the heart of our heavenly Father?'

GREGORY THE GREAT, *EPISTOLAE*, 4.31

Why is reading the Bible important?

There are many possible answers to this question; here discussion centres on what Christians believe the Bible teaches us about its own value.

The Bible reveals God

In this sense the Bible is like God's autobiography. God reveals God's actions and intentions, but also God's inner self – what drives and matters to God. As with all autobiographies, this does not mean that all there is to know about the author can be discovered. In the Bible there is still a sense of mystery about God, who remains beyond complete human understanding (see, for example, Deuteronomy 29:29; Job 42:3; Isaiah 40:28).

But the Bible does give the basis for discovering all that God considers it important for people to know now. The Bible shows God's plan of salvation, God's grace, holiness, love, justice, compassion and sovereignty. Central to God's

revelation and this plan of salvation is Jesus Christ. The New Testament presents Jesus as the fullest extent of God's revelation. People can come to know God through Jesus Christ.

The Bible offers help on the journey of faith

Christians believe that the Bible is authoritative, instructive and helpful when it comes to living their lives in response to God, just as a car manual is authoritative, instructive and helpful when it comes to running a car. The Bible provides general guidelines as well as specific ones. It is a reference point, a court of appeal for all matters relating to Christian faith.

...you have known the holy Scriptures, which are able to make you wise for salvation through faith in Christ Jesus. All Scripture is God-breathed and is useful for teaching, rebuking, correcting and training in righteousness, so that the man of God may be thoroughly equipped for every good work.'

2 TIMOTHY 3:15–17

The Creation of Adam by Michelangelo, (1510) showing God's outstretched arm imparting life to Adam. It illustrates that humankind is made in the image and likeness of God (Genesis 1:26)

*'Your word is
a lamp to my feet
and a light
for my path.'*
PSALM 119:105

*'All your words
are true; all your
righteous laws
are eternal.'*
PSALM 119:160

The Bible shows the way to live

Many sections of the Bible offer guidance about how to live. The wisdom books are particularly down to earth and instructive in this way. In fact, if you doubt whether the Bible is practically useful try reading through the book of Proverbs. The teaching of Jesus has a lot to say about how to live life in a way that is pleasing to God. The Sermon on the Mount (Matthew 5–7) addresses matters such as dealing with insults, keeping laws, managing anger and disputes, adultery in the heart, divorce, making promises, revenge, loving our enemies, giving to the poor, coping with worry, and true wisdom. When asked, 'Which is the greatest commandment in the law?' Jesus responds by stressing the importance of loving God and one's neighbour (Matthew 22:34–40). In so doing he underlines that Christian living is about putting God first and others next. This idea of self-denial becomes very important in what Jesus says about the nature of Christian discipleship (Matthew 8:34–35).

More teaching sections about Christian character and lifestyle occur in the New Testament letters (see, for example, Ephesians and James). Much of this teaching builds on Old Testament foundations, including the Ten Commandments, and on the teaching of Jesus. (See chapter 3, **Wisdom literature**; **Law**.)

The Bible brings hope for the future

Despite its relevance to the here and now, the Bible also has something to say about the future. The Bible's message is one of hope not despair. It provides a framework for thinking about this life as a small part of eternity. This life is therefore an anticipation of what is to come, bringing a hope deeper than any form of human optimism. It is hope rooted in the here and now which will reach its complete fulfilment in the future. This emphasis is particularly prominent in some of the New Testament letters, and it remains the emphasis at the Bible's end.

For the Lord himself will come down from heaven, with a loud command, with the voice of the archangel and with the trumpet call of God, and the dead in Christ will rise first. After that, we who are still alive and are left will be caught up together with them in the clouds to meet the Lord in the air. And so we will be with the Lord for ever.
1 THESSALONIANS 4:16–17

But in keeping with his promise we are looking forward to a new heaven and a new earth, the home of righteousness.
2 PETER 3:13

He who testifies to these things says, 'Yes, I am coming soon. Amen. Come, Lord Jesus.'
REVELATION 22:20

The Bible is always relevant

Christians believe that the Bible is eternally relevant because God himself is eternal, unchanging and always interacting with his creation. This is why the Bible has

Nelson Mandela, the Christian former President of South Africa, and President Barrack Obama. Obama, in his inaugural address, quoted 1 Corinthians 13:11: 'When I was a child, I used to speak like a child, think like a child, reason like a child; when I became a man, I did away with childish things.' He references this verse when he describes America as a young nation that needs to practice traits of equality and peace to define the nation.

been read throughout the years. It is not a passing fad, here today but gone tomorrow. Reading the Bible allows Christians to interact with writings that have shaped people's lives and faith ever since they were first written down and collected. Indeed the Bible still shapes lives today and will continue to do so.

The Bible brings joy and blessing to its readers

One of the compelling reasons for reading the Bible is that the Bible itself promises blessing to those who listen, understand and live by its words. See, for example, Psalm 1:

Blessed is the man
  who does not walk in the counsel
    of the wicked
  or stand in the way of sinners
  or sit in the seat of mockers.

But his delight is in the law of the Lord,
  and on his law he meditates day
    and night.

He is like a tree planted by streams
  of water,
    which yields its fruit in season
    and whose leaf does not wither.
  Whatever he does prospers.

Not so the wicked!
  They are like chaff
    that the wind blows away.

Therefore the wicked will not stand
  in the judgment,
    nor sinners in the assembly of
    the righteous.

For the Lord watches over the way of
  the righteous,
    but the way of the wicked will perish.

PSALM 1

The law from your mouth is more precious to me than thousands of pieces of silver and gold.
PSALM 119:72

For all these reasons Christians sometimes refer to the Bible as 'food' or 'bread' for people to eat. In other words, the Bible is vital to spiritual health and well-being just as eating food is vital for physical health and well-being.

Over the centuries the Christian church has adopted statements of faith to explain what it believes about the Bible. Here are a few examples:

We believe that the Word contained in these books has proceeded from God, and receives its authority from him alone, and not from human beings. And in that it is the rule of all truth, containing all that is necessary in the service of God and for our salvation, it is not lawful for anyone, even for angels, to add to it, to take away from it, or to change it. It therefore follows that no authority, whether of antiquity, or custom, or numbers, or human wisdom or judgements, or proclamations, or edicts, or decrees, or councils, or visions, or miracles, should be opposed to these Holy Scriptures, but, on the contrary, all things should be examined, regulated, and reformed, according to them.
A FRENCH CONFESSION OF FAITH
(CONFESSIO GALLICANA, 1559, ARTICLE 5)

We view the Old and New Testaments 'as containing all things necessary for salvation' and as being the rule and ultimate standard of faith.
EXTRACT FROM THE CHURCH OF ENGLAND WEBSITE:
WWW.COFE.ANGLICAN.ORG/FAITH/ANGLICAN

We believe in...

The divine inspiration and supreme authority of the Old and New Testament Scriptures, which are the written Word of God – fully trustworthy for faith and conduct.'
EVANGELICAL ALLIANCE, BASIS OF FAITH, ARTICLE 3
(2005 REVISION)

134 All Sacred Scripture is but one book, and that one book is Christ, because all divine Scripture speaks of Christ, and all divine Scripture is fulfilled in Christ.

135 The Sacred Scriptures contain the Word of God and, because they are inspired, they are truly the Word of God.

136 God is the author of Sacred Scripture because he inspired its human authors; he acts in them and by means of them. He thus gives assurance that their writings teach without error his saving truth.

137 Interpretation of the inspired Scripture must be attentive above all to what God wants to reveal through the sacred authors for our salvation. What comes from the Spirit is not fully 'understood except by the Spirit's action.'
CATECHISM OF THE CATHOLIC CHURCH, PART 1,
SECTION 1, CHAPTER 2, ARTICLE 3, 'IN BRIEF', AT
HTTP://WWW.VATICAN.VA/ARCHIVE/ENG0015/__
PT.HTM.

When Christians make Bible reading and

'But the Counsellor, the Holy Spirit, whom the Father will send in my name, will teach you all things and will remind you of everything I have said to you.'
JOHN 14:26

Christian people today embrace and value the Bible, they tap into its riches and share the passion for it which has characterized Christian communities throughout the centuries.

'Open my eyes that I may see wonderful things in your law.'
PSALM 119:18

Organizing a personal Bible reading time

Before the invention of printing presses in the fifteenth century, ordinary Christians could not read and study the Bible for themselves. Over the centuries Bibles have become more accessible, and today many Christians consider it a privilege to read the Bible for themselves. Christian people often set aside a regular time each day to read the Bible. Traditionally this has been called 'a quiet time' or 'daily devotions'; it can be any time of the day and can happen in any place. The focus of these individual times of Bible reading is on applying the insights gained from the Bible to Christians' individual lives and circumstances.

'The Christians in Berea are commended in the Bible because they "examined the Scriptures every day..." '
ACTS 17:11

Christians find it helpful to begin a devotional time by praying that the Holy Spirit will help and teach them as they read the Bible so they can understand it and apply it to their lives.

study a priority they are aligning themselves with the position that the church has given the Bible over the centuries. The Bible has been the church's resource throughout its history and the passion to preserve it and learn it has been at the heart of the life of the Christian community. When

It is always helpful to read the Bible slowly, thinking about parts that are difficult to understand, or particularly challenging or timely for some other reason. This is sometimes called 'meditating on the Bible': it does not imply some kind of mystical

One simple way to meditate or reflect carefully on the Bible is to read a short phrase a number of times and give each individual word emphasis each time, so:

I am the good shepherd.
I **am** the good shepherd.
I am **the** good shepherd.
I am the **good** shepherd.
I am the good **shepherd.**

JOHN 10:11

Anyone who listens to the word but does not do what it says is like a man who looks at his face in a mirror and, after looking at himself, goes away and immediately forgets what he looks like. But the man who looks intently into the perfect law that gives freedom, and continues to do this, not forgetting what he has heard, but doing it – he will be blessed in what he does.
JAMES 1:22–25

experience but means pondering and reflecting or thinking carefully about what you read in the Bible.

The effort put into reading the Bible in this way comes with a promise:

The Lord said to Joshua... Do not let this Book of the Law depart from your mouth; meditate on it day and night, so that you may be careful to do everything written in it. Then you will be prosperous and successful.
JOSHUA 1:1, 8

... for the gracious hand of God was on him. For Ezra had devoted himself to the study and observance of the Law of the Lord...
EZRA 7:9–10

Some Christians keep a journal or diary and record important things from their reading of the Bible so they don't forget them and can return to them later if they want to. This helps them to remember and apply the Bible to their lives.

Do not merely listen to the word, and so deceive yourselves. Do what it says.

Reading the Bible from cover to cover

Usually attempts to read the Bible from Genesis through to Revelation come to an early end! The reality is that by the time you have read the stories in Genesis and the start of Exodus you hit a lengthy section of instructions about tabernacle buildings, details about ancient civil laws of little immediate relevance to today and prolonged lists of people's names. Even the most committed readers don't find these sections an easy read! So most Bible reading plans that encourage Christians to read through their Bibles bring together texts from across the pages of Scripture. So, for example, people might read Genesis alongside a Gospel, with some psalms interspersed. This is about providing a 'balanced diet'. They read some Old Testament history; they read about Jesus; they worship God; and they think about life. Here is an example of what such a reading plan might look like:

Day 1: Genesis 1:1 – 2:25; Matthew 1:1 –

Favourite Bible verses

Here is a collection of comments made by people who were asked about their favourite Bible verses. Notice the connections they made between their chosen verses and their own lives.

My favourite Bible verse is Romans 5:8: 'But God demonstrates his own love for us in this: While we were still sinners, Christ died for us.' Because at the age of seven I realized that God didn't wait for me to be perfect – it was the first glimpse of grace that I had (although I didn't fully understand it at that time) and I have never forgotten it!

Nick, aged 32

My favourite verse is Hebrews 13:5: 'Keep your lives free from the love of money and be content with what you have, because God has said, "Never will I leave you; never will I forsake you",' because I like to think of God always being there for me. No matter what, he will never give up on me.

Sarah, aged 15

My favourite Bible verse is 'Be still and know that I am God' (Psalm 46:10) because it reminds me in the rush of life I still need to find time for God and acknowledge him.

Rachel, aged 16

My favourite Bible verses are Matthew 6:33–34: 'Seek first his kingdom and his righteousness and all these things will be given you as well. Therefore do not worry about tomorrow…' These verses help me to set my life priorities and contain a promise as well.

Rob, aged 42

My favourite Bible verse is Romans 8:28: 'And we know that in all things God works for the good of those who love him', because throughout my life this has given me strength and hope, even in the toughest times when I have not understood what has happened to me and friends around me.

Shirley, aged 74

I love reading Galatians 1:3–5: 'Grace and peace to you from God our Father and the Lord Jesus Christ, who gave himself for our sins to rescue us from the present evil age, according to the will of our God and Father, to whom be glory for ever and ever. Amen.' These verses summarize for me the hope I have as a Christian and give me joy and strength every day.

Bill, aged 73

2:12; Psalm 1:1–6; Proverbs 1:1–6
Day 2: Genesis 3:1 – 4:26; Matthew 2:13 – 3:6; Psalm 2:1–12; Proverbs 1:7–9
Day 3: Genesis 5:1 – 7:24; Matthew 3:7 – 4:11; Psalm 3:1–8; Proverbs 1:10–19
Day 4: Genesis 8:1 – 10:32; Matthew 4:12–25; Psalm 4:1–8; Proverbs 1:20–23
Day 5: Genesis 11:1 – 13:4; Matthew 5:1–26; Psalm 5:1–12; Proverbs 1:24–28

Bible reading plans

There are many reading plans that help you read through the Bible in this way. You can take as long as you like and you can choose how to design your plan. You can buy a reading plan or even sign up to an online site or email facility. If you are interested in reading the whole Bible through in one year try looking at the options available on websites such as www.oneyearbibleonline.

The Gideons:

In 1899 three commercial travellers in the USA formed an association of Christian businessmen to encourage each other in their Christian faith and to spread knowledge of God through personal evangelism and united service for the Lord Jesus Christ. They chose the name Gideons after an Old Testament leader who, with a few chosen men, did a great work for God. Today, over 250,000 members work in 181 countries, placing over 60 million copies of the Word of God annually as well as witnessing personally for Christ. Internationally over 1 billion Scriptures have been presented. Their objective is to share God's message of salvation through Jesus Christ by personal witness and through placing Bibles and New Testaments into people's hands.

www.gideons.org.uk

com and www.bibleinayear.org.

Some people still find benefits in reading the Bible straight through from Genesis to Revelation and there is no reason why you shouldn't do this if you have the perseverance required!

Alternatively you can choose a resource which selects some of the most important passages in biblical order and provides a panorama of the Bible. These can provide a Bible reading, a reflection and a question for contemplation for each day of the year. For further resources, see www.grow-with-the-bible.org.uk, wordlive.org and www.foundations21.com.

Reading the Bible chronologically

This approach to Bible reading emphasizes the order in which events in the Bible happened. For example, the book of Job is understood as describing events early in Old Testament times, so it is read with the book of Genesis rather than with Esther and Psalms according to the Bible's own order. It is worth remembering that the chronological order of events in the Bible is not always certain, so approaches can vary.

Reading the Bible thematically

Thematic Bible reading plans enable Christians to read what the Bible has to say about specific subjects. This can be useful because they can read the Bible in a way that relates specifically to the circumstances and issues they are facing in their own lives. So, for example, if they are getting married soon they may want to read what the Bible has to say about marriage and human relationships. If they are about to take on responsibility they might want to know what the Bible says about leadership. If they are suffering the pain of bereavement they might want to find comfort in the Bible. For many years a society called the Gideons has put Bibles in places such as hotel rooms, hospitals, prisons and university campuses throughout the world which include advice about how to use the Bible in various life situations. In the box opposite, you can find some examples of such advice.

Some editions of the Bible provide devotional help aimed at different groups: for example the Youth Bible, the Women's Bible, the Dad's Bible. All these attempt to outline what the Bible says about themes relevant to people today.

Bible verses I can read when...

I am afraid: Psalms 34:4; 46; Matthew 8:23–27

I am angry with other people: Ephesians 4:29–32; Colossians 3:12–14; 1 John 2:9–11

I am anxious: Isaiah 43:1–3; Philippians 4:4–7; 1 Peter 5:7

I am bereaved: Psalm 23; Matthew 5:4; John 11:21–27; 1 Thessalonians 4:13–18; Revelation 21:1–5

I am aware of failure and sin: Psalm 51; Luke 15:11–24; Romans 5:8

I feel God is far away: Psalm 139:1–18; John 10:29; James 4:8

I need guidance: Psalm 32:8; Proverbs 3:5–6; Luke 6:12–13; Acts 15:28

I am ill: Romans 8:18–25; 2 Corinthians 12:9

I am lonely: Psalm 73:23–24; Isaiah 41:10; John 14:15–21

I need peace: Isaiah 26:3; John 14:27; Romans 5:1–5; Philippians 4:4–7

I am tempted: Matthew 26:39–41; Romans 6:1–14; 1 Corinthians 10:13; Hebrews 4:15–16

I am tired: Isaiah 40:28–31; Matthew 11:28–31

I am weak: Joshua 1:6–9; Isaiah 12:2; Hebrews 4:15–16; 2 Timothy 1:7

Psalms that can help you when you are feeling...

abandoned: 22, 27, 31, 38, 41, 42

afraid: 27, 34, 46, 55, 56, 91

angry: 4, 37, 73, 109

bereaved: 23, 27, 71, 116

betrayed: 41, 52, 55

burnt out: 63, 102

confused: 12, 73, 107

depressed: 6, 25, 27, 42, 43, 143

despairing: 13, 42, 130, 142

discouraged: 16, 23, 31, 34, 40, 43, 55, 61, 93, 121

doubting: 10, 14, 27, 53, 77

far from God: 13, 16, 22, 27, 42, 107, 139

guilty: 25, 32, 38, 51, 103, 130

helpless: 10, 27, 42, 46, 71, 121

hurt: 71, 109, 120

ill or weak: 6, 22, 31, 38, 41, 42, 69, 73, 102, 103

impatient: 13, 37, 40, 62

insecure: 11, 16, 27, 37, 46, 63, 71, 91, 93, 125, 136

jealous: 37, 40, 73

joyful: 8, 19, 33, 47, 66, 92, 103

lonely: 3, 10, 13, 25, 40, 102, 139, 142

overwhelmed: 9, 24, 61, 69, 72, 142

proud: 12, 36, 49

self-confident: 14, 75

sleepless: 3, 4, 63, 77

stressed: 11, 25, 31, 62, 141, 142

stubborn: 32, 95, 107

tempted: 38, 51, 141

thankful: 34, 100, 116, 136, 138

threatened: 3, 7, 9, 28, 31, 35, 57, 70, 71

trapped: 25, 27, 31, 88, 118

troubled: 4, 10, 20, 27, 34, 40, 46, 102, 120

undecided: 1, 5, 23, 25, 32, 37, 125, 127

weary: 57, 69, 116

worried: 23, 37, 46, 57

My favourite way of reading the Bible is...

Today there are more ways than ever to read the Bible: some Christians have Bible text calendars from which they can read a verse each day; others have verses texted to their mobile phones or emailed to their computers.

I'm reading the Bible with the help of my youth leader. We discuss our reading every Thursday night and this helps to make things clearer and I have someone to ask about verses I find difficult or confusing.

Will, aged 14

I am reading my Bible with the help of the church lectionary. This gives me a good variety of readings and helps me to appreciate the shape of the Christian year.

Rob, aged 42

At the moment I am reading my Bible with the help of 'Bible in a Year'. This is helping me because it is in chronological order so you get everything in context. Also it is broken up into an Old Testament reading, a psalm, a proverb and a New Testament reading and I love this variety.

Joanna, aged 17

Help reading the Bible

There are many tools that can help with reading the Bible, from many different perspectives. Some of these are particularly useful when you first begin to read the Bible; others will help at later stages on the journey.

Bible reading notes

Bible reading notes are often arranged into sections by date to encourage a regular daily discipline of Bible reading. They usually take a short passage of Scripture and offer some explanation about the context, meaning and application of the selected text. Points of particular interest or difficulty are clarified. These notes often have a devotional focus, providing a point to reflect on personally or suggesting a few words that can be used as a prayer. Sometimes they also include suggestions about something to do as a means of responding to Scripture. Bible reading notes of this kind are very popular with Christians who wish to spend a few minutes every day reading their Bible. (See **Further reading suggestions** at the end of this chapter for recommendations of Bible reading notes.)

Study guides

Study guides are half-way between reading notes and commentaries. They are relatively lightweight, but try to give readers the opportunity to delve more deeply into Bible passages while still maintaining a practical edge by explaining the implications of the Bible for everyday Christian life. Rather than dividing Bible texts into daily readings, they are organized around the structure of the texts themselves. For this reason some sections are longer than other sections and often they contain more introductory background material. Readers need to work out for themselves how much time they will devote to each section of the biblical text. These study guides are often specifically designed for use in Bible study groups and discussions. (See **Further reading suggestions** at the end of this chapter for recommended study guides.)

Commentaries

There are very many commentaries on the Bible available in bookshops, libraries and online. They have been produced throughout the history of Christianity. Commentaries, as the name suggests, offer comment on the biblical text and usually include an analysis of the structure and meaning of the text too. They provide information about the setting, context and significance of a text. This helps Christians to make appropriate judgments about the text and its relevance for them today. Such judgments are a very important part of the work of a preacher and for this reason commentaries have an important place in a minister's study.

Questions to ask when studying the Bible:

◆ **Context:** What is the historical setting? What surrounds the passage?

◆ **Form:** What type of literature is it?

◆ **Structure:** How is the passage designed?

◆ **Theme:** What are the main ideas and words?

◆ **Meaning:** What did the passage mean then and what does it mean now?

Sometimes commentaries can be rather technical and overwhelming, but there are some accessible series as well as the more academic ones. (See **Further reading**

Jesus' conversation with Nicodemus (3:1–15)

The evangelist introduces Nicodemus: *Now there was a man of the Pharisees named Nicodemus, a member of the Jewish ruling council.* As 'a man of the Pharisees', Nicodemus was a member of the most influential Jewish sect in Jesus' time. The Pharisees are mentioned twenty times in the Gospel of John, and are nearly always portrayed as antagonistic to Jesus. The only exceptions are here in 3:1, where Nicodemus the Pharisee comes to Jesus, and 9:16, where some of the Pharisees are bold enough to ask how Jesus could do miraculous signs if he were a sinner.

Nicodemus is also described as 'a member of the Jewish ruling council', or Sanhedrin. Members of the Sanhedrin are also generally presented as antagonistic towards Jesus in this Gospel. Apart from 3:1ff., the one exception is found in 12:42, where the evangelist says 'Yet at the same time many even among the leaders (lit. 'rulers') believed in him. But because of the Pharisees they would not confess their faith for fear they would be put out of the synagogue.'

COLIN G. KRUSE, *TYNDALE NEW TESTAMENT COMMENTARY: JOHN*, DOWNERS GROVE: INTERVARSITY PRESS, 2008, P. 106.

Christ Talks with Nicodemus, (1886–94), by James Tissot.

Bible reading throughout the world

The Bible Society distributes more than 600 million copies of the Bible every year but advertise statistics such as:

- 4,500 languages still wait for even one book of the Bible.
- One billion people haven't learned to read – but only 3 per cent of languages have the Bible in audio.
- Someone goes blind every five seconds – but the Bible exists in Braille in only thirty languages.

suggestions at the end of this chapter.)

Reference books

When reading the Bible, it is particularly helpful to have to hand a good Bible atlas and dictionary. These can help you to understand the geographical, historical and archaeological references in the text as well as to identify some of the key terms and people who figure in it. This book is one resource you can use, but there are other more specialist works too (see **Further reading suggestions** at the end of this chapter).

Reading the Bible with other people

As well as reading the Bible individually, Christians consider reading the Bible with other people very important. This happens when the Bible is read publicly in church, often followed by a sermon or homily. In addition many small Bible study groups are arranged for church members and these are particularly important for encouragement and mutual learning. Today churches are experimenting with new schemes such as Bible reading partners and Bible book clubs. The idea of these groups is to introduce a level of support and accountability to help with the sometimes challenging discipline of Bible reading. All these initiatives show the importance to Christian people of reading the Bible, while also emphasizing the advantages of mutual growth and support in this discipline of the Christian life.

Further reading suggestions

Bible reading notes

Scripture Union notes: for example *Daily Bread*, *Closer to God* and *Encounter with God*.

Crusade for World Revival (CWR) publications: *Every Day with Jesus* and *Cover to Cover Every Day*.

Bible Reading Fellowship (BRF): *New Daylight Day by Day with God*.

InterVarsity Press: *Search the Scriptures* and *This Morning with God*.

Study guides

The Crossway Bible Guides (Leicester: Crossway Books) cover a range of Bible books and are written by various authors (see, for example, *Acts*, by Stephen Gaukroger (1997); *Timothy and Titus*, by Michael Griffiths (1996); and *Ruth and Esther*, by Debra Reid (2000).

Spring Harvest (www. springharvest.org) and the Keswick Convention (www. keswickministries.org) also produce similar Bible guides.

Commentaries

The following commentary series contain volumes on most or all Bible books:

The Bible Speaks Today series (InterVarsity Press).

The Interpretation Series (John Knox Press).

The NIV Application Commentary (Zondervan).

The Tyndale Commentary (InterVarsity Press).

Bibliography and further resources

The following books all introduce aspects of the Bible:

Mike Beaumont, *The One-Stop Bible Guide*, Oxford: Lion, 2006.

John Drane, *Introducing the Old Testament*, Oxford: Lion, 1986.

John Drane, *Introducing the New Testament*, Oxford: Lion, 1986.

Gordon Fee and Douglas Stuart, *How to Read the Bible for All its Worth*, London: Scripture Union, 1993.

Caroline Mason and Pat Alexander (eds), *A Treasury of Bible Pictures*, Lion, 1987.

Nick Page, *The One-Stop Bible Atlas*, Oxford: Lion, 2010.

Pheme Perkins, *Reading the New Testament*, Mahwah: Paulist Press, 1988.

Joseph Rhymer, *Atlas of the Biblical World*, London: Hamlyn, 1982.

Martin Selman and Martin Manser, *Collins Dictionary of the Bible*, New York: HarperCollins, 2005.

IVP Dictionaries of the Bible (for example *The Pentateuch*; *Jesus and the Gospels*; *Paul and His Letters*), Downers Grove: InterVarsity Press, 1992–2008.

Notes

Chapter 1

1. Extract from a transcript of the Coronation ceremony of Queen Elizabeth II of Great Britain when the Archbishop of Canterbury presented her with a copy of the Bible.
2. Although there is no evidence of the preservation of Esther by the Qumran community, the survival of the Esther text points to its preservation by other Jewish communities during this time.

Chapter 2

1. It is important to remember that all dates here are approximate and only a few are universally agreed or can be established with reasonable precision. Having said that, it is impossible to look at the Bible's historical setting without using some dates as a guideline and so, while their imprecision is recognized, dates are used.

Chapter 3

1. The prophet Isaiah is linked to different historical periods in this table. This is because the Old Testament book that bears his name is sometimes understood to be a compilation of prophecies that emerged over a period of time, with only the first thirty-nine chapters emerging in the lifetime of the eighth-century BC prophet Isaiah.

Chapter 4

1. This is a different Darius from the king of the Persians who succeeded Cyrus and who is mentioned in Ezra. His historicity is uncertain.

Chapter 9

1. The chapter headings here are taken from Alister McGrath, *Christian Theology: An Introduction*, Oxford: Blackwell, 1994.
2. This is a sub-section heading within one of McGrath's chapters.
3. This approach to theology has been proposed and discussed in more detail in J. Colwell, *Rhythm of Doctrine*, Paternoster, 2007. The following section is a brief résumé of some elements of Dr Colwell's thesis.
4. The identification of seasons used here follows the order and names of seasons suggested in The European Province of the Society of Saint Francis, *Celebrating Common Prayer: A Version of the Daily Office SSF*, Mowbray, 1992. While other versions of the Daily Office exist there is an agreed uniformity in the basic structure of the church year.

Glossary

Megiddo was a city on the southern side of the plain of Esdraelon (in modern Israel) where it commanded the most important pass to the Mediterranean coast: it was the site of one of the Israelites' greatest victories (Judges 5:19).

apostle

From the Greek meaning 'one who is sent', the term refers primarily to the twelve disciples whom Jesus sent out in the power of the Spirit to take the gospel to the world. Their basic qualification was that they had been with Jesus during his earthly ministry and had witnessed his resurrection. Others were added to their number, such as Paul (1 Corinthians 15:7–9; Acts 14:4; Galatians 1:19) and Matthias, who replaced Judas Iscariot. The apostles are recognized as the founders of the church, comparable in status with the prophets of the Old Testament, because of their authoritative teaching of the gospel and establishing of new churches. The word 'apostle' is also used more generally to refer to a representative or messenger of a particular church (2 Corinthians 8:23; Philippians 2:25).

Ark of the Covenant

A box placed between two cherubim in the Most Holy Place in the **tabernacle** and later the **Temple**. It contained the tablets of the Ten Commandments, a jar of the manna that God had given the Israelites to eat in the desert (Exodus 16:14–15) and Aaron's staff, which God had miraculously caused to bud, blossom and bear fruit (Numbers 17). The reality of God's holy presence could make the Ark dangerous for the unwary (1 Samuel 5:1 – 7:1; 2 Samuel 6:6–15), but primarily it symbolized the blessing of God's presence among the people and God's commitment to God's covenant promises.

Armageddon

Armageddon, which means 'mountain of Megiddo', is the place that represents God's final victory over God's enemies (Revelation 16:16).

ascension

The term 'ascension' is applied to the moment when the resurrected Jesus was taken up to heaven in the clouds (Acts 1:9–11), from where he poured his Spirit on the **church** at Pentecost, ten days later. An angel told the watching disciples that Jesus' **second coming** would take place in the same manner as his ascension. Though the ascension is described in physical terms because Jesus had a physical body, its main significance for Christians is to show that Jesus was exalted to ultimate authority in heaven because he had completed his work on earth.

baptism

The word is originally a Greek term meaning 'dipping or immersing in water'. The practice of baptism originated in Jewish ceremonial washings, but it was through John the Baptist that it became a central feature of church life. Surprisingly, baptism does not seem to have been a major feature of Jesus' ministry, though his disciples did baptize on his behalf (John 4:2). John the Baptist taught baptism as a sign of repentance, and Jesus submitted to John's baptism as an act of solidarity with sinners as well as a mark of his own commitment to God's will (Matthew 3:11–17). The early **church** adopted baptism on Jesus' own instruction (Mark 16:16) as an expression of a person's initial commitment to Christ in **faith** and repentance. The phrase 'in/into the name of' indicates entry into a relationship of belonging to God (Matthew 28:19). Baptism is also closely associated with the gift of the Holy Spirit and with the idea of union with Christ, as the description of a believer's death and resurrection in Romans 6:3–4 powerfully suggests.

church

In the Bible, this term refers to a group of people committed to Jesus Christ rather than to an institution or a building: 'church' is the New Testament term for the people of God. It extends the Old Testament concept of Israel as the people of God, and many of the descriptions of Israel found in the Old Testament, such as God's bride (Isaiah 62:5) and God's flock (Psalm 95:7), are also applied to the church (Acts 20:28–29; Ephesians 5:25–32). The church comprises those who follow Jesus as **messiah** and Lord, whatever their background, and the New Testament emphasizes their unity in the faith much more than the emerging differences between churches. The idea of unity is also reflected in other metaphors for the church, such as the body of Christ, God's household or family, and God's building or temple.

The church is universal, regional and local. Its wider unity is sometimes expressed in practical terms, such as through Paul's collection of alms in Greece and Asia Minor for the support of poor Christians in Jerusalem. The Bible is remarkably quiet about forms of church government, leaving local churches with some freedom to develop their own structures. Rather, emphasis is placed on the need for leaders to be gifted by God and of good character, and on church members taking their responsibilities seriously. The basic features of early church life were fellowship, teaching, prayer and breaking of bread or the Lord's Supper (Acts 2:42), and new converts were brought into the church through **baptism**.

The church exists to be God's people in the world (1 Peter 2:9–10), with a twofold responsibility towards God and towards unbelievers. In relation to God, the church is to praise God and to live in union with Christ through the power of the Spirit. In relation to the world, the church is to take the gospel to every nation in order to make new disciples of Christ. To this end, Jesus poured out his Spirit on the church at Pentecost so that they could be his witnesses to the ends of the earth (Acts 1:8).

Communion, *see* Lord's Supper

Council of Nicaea

This church council was a gathering of church representatives responsible for safeguarding the **faith**: it was held in AD 325 and was significant because of the wide area from which representatives came. Theologically it was concerned with establishing the divinity of Christ and the Holy Spirit in response to an early heresy (Arianism) that held that Jesus Christ was not the eternally divine Son of God. The council agreed the statements, later enshrined in the Nicene Creed (see chapter 9), that Jesus Christ is the Son, was 'begotten, not made' and is 'of the same substance with the Father'.

Council of Trent

This was the first council called by the Roman Catholic Church following the Reformation. It met in three stages between 1545 and 1563. It was concerned with matters relating to Roman Catholic doctrines and practices. It produced an important catechism and, in 1546, added to the Roman Catholic Old Testament twelve books from the Apocrypha (see chapter 2).

day of the Lord

This is a Hebrew expression referring to a time when God acts and reveals himself in a particularly significant way. In origin it is associated with God helping Israel in their battles to occupy the Promised Land, and because of this it became a symbol of Israel's hope that God would finally intervene on their behalf (Amos 5:18–20). But the prophets warned that God would act to fulfil God's own purposes rather than the people's expectations and that the day would be one of judgment as well as **salvation**. Their threats were fulfilled when both Israel and Judah fell. In the New Testament, the term describes the time when Jesus Christ will be fully revealed at his return to remove all forms of evil and finally establish his eternal kingdom. This event will be accompanied by signs throughout the natural world, and Christians are warned to be ready at any time.

disciple

'Disciple' is a New Testament term meaning 'a learner or pupil', and used both for the twelve **apostles** and for believers in general (Matthew 10:1; Luke 6:13). It is also applied to the followers of people other than Jesus, including John the Baptist and the Pharisees (see chapter 7). The word 'discipleship' does not occur in the Bible, but is frequently used in later Christian writing to refer to the way of life expected of those who follow Jesus. The theme is especially common in the Gospels, where Jesus explains that following him involves committing one's whole life to God. Jesus is the model for discipleship, with the cross as its symbol (Mark 8:34–35) and his servanthood its pattern (Mark 10:42–45). However, discipleship also brings the blessings of the kingdom of God, both in this life and in the life to come (Mark 10:28–30).

eschatology, *see* last things

Eucharist, *see* Lord's Supper

exile

Exile was the consequence of the collapse of the kingdoms of Israel and Judah in 722 and 587 BC; their inhabitants were taken to Assyria and Babylonia respectively. The experience of exile is understood as God punishing the people for their persistent rejection of God's will, and as the fulfilment of God's covenant threats (2 Kings 17:7–23; 2 Chronicles 36:15–20). The Babylonian exile formally ended with Cyrus's edict in 539/8 BC permitting the Jews to return home (Ezra 1:1–4), but many families either took several decades to make up their minds to do so – or never returned at all (see chapter 4, **The nation in exile**). The whole experience had a profound effect on the Jews, many of whom remained scattered across the nations, either because of their discouragement or because living in the Promised Land no longer had the same significance for them. However, the exile was also a formative period, when prophets such as Jeremiah and Ezekiel were active and, according to many scholars, the editing of the so-called Deuteronomic history (Joshua, Judges, 1 and 2 Samuel and 1 and 2 Kings) was finally completed. The emergence of these Old Testament books helped the Jews to understand God's ways in the exile and provided them with fresh hope, for both the immediate and the more long-term future (Jeremiah 30–33).

faith

Several kinds of faith are mentioned in the Bible, but it is essentially an attitude of mind and heart by which a person entrusts himself or herself to God. A definition from the Bible itself is that 'faith is being sure of what we hope for and certain of what we do not see' (Hebrews 11:1). This verse refers to the object of faith as the unseen God and God's promises, especially concerning Jesus Christ (John 14:1); the effect of such faith is a deep assurance about God and God's ability to keep these promises. The experience of faith begins with 'saving faith'; that is, a complete trust in Jesus Christ that he can make a person right with God through his death on the cross. Faith of this kind is often contrasted with an attempt to gain acceptance with God through human pride and achievement (Romans 3:21–28). Such faith is demonstrated throughout Old Testament history (Hebrews 11), and is possible for anyone, irrespective of his or her background. Faith is expected to develop in each believer so that it becomes a way of life (Galatians 2:20). The genuineness of a person's faith is also shown by the extent to which he or she obeys God. Verbal claims to faith are worthless unless they are supported by appropriate actions (James 2:14–26).

In addition to the life of faith, the New

Testament mentions a special gift of faith (1 Corinthians 12:9), which can be exercised on occasions of particular need such as severe illness (Acts 3:1–10) or famine (1 Kings 17:2–6). Although faith is a human attribute, the ability to believe is ultimately God's gift (Ephesians 2:8–9). God provides faith to those who ask, but it is also stimulated by hearing and reading God's word (Romans 10:14–17).

Finally, faith is sometimes understood as the basic objective core of Christian belief, especially in the phrase 'the faith' (Jude 3).

fall

'The fall' is the term used by theologians to describe the first sin and its consequences (Genesis 3). First, the idea of a fall assumes that God created a perfect world before Adam and Eve disobeyed God's command about not eating the fruit of the tree of the knowledge of good and evil (see chapter 6, **Adam and Eve**). Secondly, it recognizes that, as a result of that one sin, human life has changed irrevocably and that the world continues under the pain and suffering of God's curse. Paul explains that all human beings have become sinners and are subject to death (Romans 5:12–14). Under the influence of Augustine, in particular, this led to the development of the doctrine of original sin, according to which every person is born inherently sinful. Thirdly, the fall of the human race is associated with the fall of the devil and his angels from heaven (Revelation 12:9), but whereas the final destruction of Satan and his angels is certain, Christ is able to set human beings free from all the effects of the fall.

gifts of the Spirit, *see* spiritual gifts

grace

'Grace' means 'God's undeserved favour to all'. It is partly demonstrated by God's reluctance to judge people for their sins, as reflected in the description of God as 'slow to anger' (Exodus 34:6). However, the primary mark of God's grace is the sending of God's Son Jesus Christ as Saviour. Though human beings are by nature opposed to the gospel (Romans 5:8), God provides further grace so that they can accept Christ's love for them (Ephesians 2:8–9). Grace is sometimes contrasted with law (Romans 6:14), but in fact the relationship between the two involves a delicate balance. Paul makes a double contrast between legalism and God's grace, and between Old Testament Law and the gospel as a basis for acceptance with God (Galatians 3:18–25). But neither of these means that grace and Law are opposed to each other. God's gift of the Law to Israel was an act of grace, and God gives grace to God's people to follow the Law. This means that the grace God gives Christians enables them to do what God requires and does not absolve them of the responsibility of obeying God's will (2 Peter 3:18).

incarnation

This is the belief that the eternal God took on human, bodily form in the person of Jesus Christ. The term is an attempt to do justice to the biblical teaching that Jesus was both fully divine and fully human, despite the difficulty of such a view from the perspective of either logic or traditional monotheism. The word 'incarnation' comes from the Latin, meaning 'in flesh', and emphasizes that Jesus came in the flesh; that is, that he had a physical human body (John 1:14; 1 Timothy 3:16).

Jerome *see* Vulgate

justification

Justification is the work of God by which God makes and declares people 'just' or 'righteous'. This action is at the heart of the Christian gospel, since without Christ no one can be justified before God. Justification is basically a legal concept, and refers to a person's status in a court of law rather than to his or her moral character. It was achieved by Jesus dying as a representative of the unrighteous: 'Christ died for sins once for all, the righteous for the unrighteous, to bring you to God' (1 Peter 3:18). The resurrection is the vindication of all that Christ achieved by his death. Justification is therefore a gift of God which a person receives by putting faith in Christ rather than in human achievements (Romans 3:21–31), and its reality in a person's life is shown by keeping God's requirements. The consequences of the New Testament understanding of justification were revolutionary, although, as Paul shows, it was hardly new since it went right back to Abraham (Romans 4). Since faith is available to anyone, whether Jew or Gentile, justification by faith becomes the basis of belonging to the people of God.

kingdom of God

This is a central idea in the teaching of Jesus, especially in the **Synoptic Gospels**, for which Matthew generally uses the expression 'kingdom of heaven'. God's kingdom is about God's rule both in heaven and on earth. The idea goes back to the exodus (Exodus 19:6), though the main Old Testament references occur in the Psalms and the prophets (Psalm 103:19; Obadiah 21). These scriptures encouraged many Jewish people to look forward to God's decisive intervention in Israel's favour, but Jesus demonstrated, especially through his parables and **miracles**, that the benefits of God's kingdom were available to all who believed in him. Jesus taught that God's kingdom was inseparable from himself; this was the main new feature in Jesus' teaching. The powerful presence of God was demonstrated by his miracles and by his bringing good news to the poor (Matthew 11:2–6, echoing the promise of Isaiah 35:5–6; 61:1). Since his death, resurrection and **ascension**, Christians believe that Jesus has reigned from God's throne in heaven. The early church proclaimed the good news that Jesus had been exalted to

kingly rule after his suffering and death, and they looked forward to the full revelation of God's kingdom at Jesus' **second coming** (Acts 28:31; 1 Corinthians 15:24–25; Revelation 11:15).

Last Supper, *see* Lord's Supper

last things

The last things is one of the Bible's most important themes, also known as eschatology (from the Greek word *eschatos* meaning 'last'). The central idea is that history is moving towards a climax as a result of God's plan for the world. This process begins with God's work in creation, which looks forward to a future completion (Genesis 1:28; 2:15–17); and it is developed in many Old Testament promises. The clearest Old Testament account comes from the prophets' descriptions of the 'last days', when all forms of evil and sin will be removed and God's original intentions for the human race will be restored. Isaiah even refers to 'new heavens and a new earth' – a new creation (Isaiah 65:17; 66:22).

Jesus taught that this final plan, which he called the **kingdom of God**, had arrived (Mark 1:15). The evidence was to be seen in his **miracles**, his teaching and especially his death and resurrection. However, Jesus also spoke about a future kingdom (Mark 13:26), illustrating one of the most important features of New Testament teaching: that the last days are already present as well as being expected in the future. The former aspect must be held in tension with future hope if justice is to be done to the biblical idea.

God's kingdom will be completed at Jesus' second coming, when the present world will be destroyed and replaced (Revelation 21–22). Those who have opposed God, including the devil and his angels, will suffer final judgment and be excluded from God's presence for ever. Those with **faith** in Jesus, however, will come into all the blessings of heaven. They will be transformed by resurrection and enabled to enjoy eternal life in the presence of Jesus (1 Corinthians 15).

laying on of hands

This is a symbolic action for the provision of God's blessing, especially in healing (Luke 4:40), or for setting a person apart for God's service (Acts 13:3). It could also symbolize the transfer of sins to a sacrificial animal (Leviticus 16:21), perhaps indicating ownership of the animal (Leviticus 4:4).

lectionary

A term that simply means a scheme of readings from the Bible that allows Scripture to be read in public worship over a particular period in an ordered and systematic way. Such schemes have been used in the **church** from its early days. The use of a lectionary assumes a commitment to regularly recalling the story of God's dealings with God's people. Using a lectionary that is common throughout the world is also a means of expressing a local church's place in the worldwide church.

Lord's Supper

The Bible's term (1 Corinthians 11:20) for Holy Communion or the Eucharist. 'Holy Communion' emphasizes the idea of a fellowship or communion meal (1 Corinthians 10:16), while 'Eucharist' (which means 'thanksgiving') comes from the practice of giving thanks (1 Corinthians 11:24). The Lord's Supper is based on the meal that Jesus ate with his disciples the night before he died (Matthew 26:26–29). Through his 'words of institution', however, Jesus transformed an Old Testament practice (the Passover meal) into a celebration of the new covenant. These words may be understood as symbolic of Jesus' death on the cross; but Roman Catholics, Orthodox Christians and some members of other churches hold that the bread and wine of the Eucharist actually change into the substance of Jesus' body and blood. The Christian practice of taking bread and wine was originally part of a larger meal known as the 'breaking of bread' (Acts 2:42) or 'love feast'

(Jude 12), but its significance is disputed by scholars.

Maccabean uprising

After years of being subjected to the powers that surrounded them, the Jews eventually rebelled against a Seleucid leader called Antiochus IV Epiphanes (175–164 BC), who had tried to impose Greek culture on the Jewish people. The rebellion began in 167 BC and, after three years of war, the Jews took control of Jerusalem and cleansed the **Temple**, which Antiochus had defiled by sacrificing swine at a pagan altar. (See chapter 5, **Before the birth of Jesus**.)

messiah

'Messiah' is a term based on a Hebrew word meaning 'an anointed person', and equivalent to the Greek word *christos*, from which 'Christ' derives. It usually describes a long-awaited deliverer who would finally establish God's kingdom and destroy God's enemies. A sense of expectation of the messiah is clearly evident in the New Testament (Luke 3:15). In the Old Testament, however, the word is rarely used, and refers to various anointed leaders such as kings or priests (Psalm 2:2; Daniel 9:25) rather than a future saviour.

Although Jesus' disciples eventually recognized him as the expected messiah, Jesus generally avoided the title because most of his contemporaries were looking for a king descended from David who would free Israel from Roman oppression. Because Jesus saw his messiahship in terms of suffering and death, in the tradition of Old Testament accounts such as that of the Suffering Servant (Isaiah 52:13 – 53:12), many first century AD Jews could not accept him as messiah.

Belief in Jesus as messiah became the central feature of the **church**'s gospel, which spoke of him as the crucified and risen messiah (Acts 2:36; 17:3).

miracles

Miracles form an important part of the biblical record, though they usually occur in association with major events rather than in isolation. They are connected with critical periods such as the exodus from Egypt or the threat to Israel during the time of Elijah and Elisha, but they occur above all in the life of Jesus. The frequency and authority of Jesus' miracles and their integral relation to his ministry exceed all other instances of miracle-working in the Bible. The supreme miracle is Jesus' resurrection, which forms the climax of the gospel (Acts 2:22–36).

Miracles are never presented as proof of God's existence or power. Jesus recognized that **faith** based on miracle-working is shallow and is distinct from saving faith (John 2:23–25). One reason for this is that miracle-working is not limited to those who believe in the God of the Bible (Exodus 7:10–13; Matthew 7:22). Rather, biblical miracles are signs pointing to the nature of God and of God's purposes. Many of Jesus' miracles, for example, were signs of God's compassion for those who suffer or of the special nature of Jesus' mission.

patriarchs

This is a collective term for Abraham and his most significant descendants: Isaac, Jacob and Joseph. It implies they are the fathers of Israelite religion. Genesis 12–50 is often referred to as 'the patriarchal narratives'.

providence

This word is used to refer to God's loving provision of the good things of life for everyone, along with God's often unseen work in human history to fulfil God's purposes. A belief in providence assumes that God is active throughout the world as well as in the church, and that God is constantly engaged in looking after people's physical and spiritual needs (Matthew 5:45; James 1:17). Many examples are given in the Bible of God providing for individuals and communities, as an encouragement to trust in God in difficult circumstances (Genesis 45:5–11; 1 Kings 17:1–9). The idea of providence takes human freedom fully into account, and allows that God works through suffering rather than removing it. It also underlines that God will ultimately achieve God's intention to establish God's kingdom (Revelation 11:15).

Purim

This is a Jewish festival established to celebrate the Jews' miraculous deliverance from the threat of a widespread massacre in the Persian period (Esther 9:20–28) (see chapter 6, **Esther**). The name comes from the word *pur*, meaning 'lot', since the festival's date in the twelfth month was originally selected by lot.

Reformation

'Reformation' is the term applied to a movement that effected profound religious changes in Europe in the sixteenth century. It began in Germany with Martin Luther, an Augustinian monk who became a Doctor of Theology and Professor of Scripture at Wittenberg University in 1512. Though originally loyal to the Catholic Church he was horrified by some of its corrupt practices, especially the selling of indulgences (church documents remitting some or all of the penance for a person's sins). He produced a critique in the form of his Ninety-Five Theses, which he pinned to the door of Wittenberg Castle church on 31 October 1517 (still celebrated as 'Reformation Day' in Germany). The reformers wanted the church to re-establish its commitment to holiness, preaching, evangelism and high standards of moral behaviour. The Reformation led to the establishment of the first Protestant churches as well as far-reaching changes within the Roman Catholic Church.

sabbath

'Sabbath' is a Hebrew word meaning 'rest'. The

Old Testament laws required rest from ordinary work every seventh day and allowing fields to lie fallow every seventh or sabbatical year (Exodus 23:10–12). By the first century AD, observing the sabbath had become an important mark of being a Jew, though the original concept of enjoyment and restoration was submerged in tradition (Matthew 12:1–14). The sabbath was less significant for the early **church**, who celebrated the first day of the week, being the day of Jesus' resurrection, rather than the Jewish sabbath (Acts 20:7).

saints

In the Bible 'saints' is a term meaning 'holy people', used in reference to the people of God. In the New Testament it is a synonym for 'Christians' (Romans 1:7). The modern sense of a saint as an especially holy individual who has been formally recognized as such developed gradually in the early church.

salvation

Salvation has sometimes been identified as the unifying theme in the Bible as a whole. It is presented in the form of a story that describes the working out of God's eternal plan to deal with the problem of human sin. The story is set against the background of the history of God's people and reaches its climax in the person and work of Christ. The Old Testament part of the story shows that people are sinners by nature, and describes a series of covenants by which God sets people free and makes promises to them. God's plan includes the promise of a blessing for all nations through Abraham and the redemption of Israel from every form of bondage. God showed God's saving power throughout Israel's history, but also spoke to the prophets about a messianic figure who would save all people from the power, guilt and penalty of sin. Christians believe that this role was fulfilled by Jesus, who will ultimately destroy suffering, pain, and death (1 John 3:8). Jesus will finally replace the present evil world with new heavens and new earth over which he will reign for ever.

Alongside this story is an emphasis on the need for individual salvation. According to the New Testament, salvation is a gift from God which anyone may receive by exercising **faith** in Christ and repentance for their sin (Acts 20:21). Through salvation, people become new creations in Christ (2 Corinthians 5:17); their sins are forgiven; they receive eternal life and become children of God. They also receive the Holy Spirit, who enables them to live a new life based on God's requirements and to spread the gospel to others (Acts 1:8; 2:38).

The basis of salvation is the person and work of Jesus. Though these are described in many ways, they centre on his roles as the **messiah** or Christ who fulfilled the Old Testament and as the Lamb of God who died to take away the sin of the world (John 1:29). Jesus' resurrection vindicates his death, and his victory is confirmed by his exaltation to God's throne. For this reason, the New Testament portrays Jesus as the only saviour of human beings (Acts 4:12) and the early **church** regarded his salvation as a message for everyone, Gentiles as well as Jews (Acts 13:47).

sanctification

This term implies the setting apart of somebody or something for God. It has two main emphases among its various meanings in the New Testament, referring either to believers being made fit for God's holy presence (1 Corinthians 6:9–11) or to the process by which believers' lives are morally and spiritually transformed through the Holy Spirit (1 Peter 1:2). It can also be used to mean setting someone or something apart for God's service (Matthew 23:17; John 17:17, 19), or for having a godly influence on someone (1 Corinthians 7:14).

second coming, see last things

Septuagint

The Septuagint is the translation of the Old Testament into Greek, named after the Greek word for seventy. The name was given because of a legend according to which the translation was made in seventy days by seventy scholars who, locked away separately from one another, miraculously produced seventy exactly identical translations. In reality the translation was done book by book by anonymous people over a period of at least a hundred years in the third and second centuries BC, probably in the region of the Egyptian metropolis of Alexandria. Later it was used by many of the earliest Christians, for example when New Testament authors quote from the Scriptures. It can often be established whether the Hebrew Bible or the Septuagint is being quoted in the New Testament because the Septuagint is not always a literal translation but contains some interpretative bias and shows influences of the contemporary culture.

Synoptic Gospels

This is a collective term used for the first three Gospels in the New Testament: Matthew, Mark and Luke. They have so much in common that they are called Synoptic, meaning 'the ones with the same perspective'. The Gospel of John offers a different perspective and style in its presentation of the life and ministry of Jesus Christ.

tabernacle

The tabernacle was the tent in which God was worshipped from Moses' time until Solomon's (Exodus 25–27). It was also called the Tent of Meeting or the Tent of the Testimony. Originally made for use in the wilderness as the Israelites travelled from place to place, it also served as Israel's main place of worship in the Promised Land. Even there, it seems to have moved from one site to another, and was used finally at Gibeon before the **Temple** in Jerusalem replaced it (2 Chronicles 1:5).

Temple

Three successive temples were built in Jerusalem for worshipping the Lord. Solomon built the first one, but it was destroyed by the Babylonians in 587 BC and had to be replaced after the Jews returned from the **exile**. The Temple of the New Testament period was built by Herod the Great but not completed until AD 64, just before the Romans destroyed it in AD 70.

transfiguration

This term is used of the significant moment, recorded in the **Synoptic Gospels**, when Jesus, accompanied by Moses and Elijah, shone with the glory of God. It emphasizes the close link between Christ's ministry and Old Testament revelation, and anticipates what Jesus would achieve through his death and resurrection. God's voice, identifying Jesus as the Son of God, confirmed Peter's earlier acknowledgment of Jesus' messiahship (Matthew 16:13–17; 17:1–8).

Vulgate

From Latin *vulgatus* ('common'), this is the name given to the Latin translation of the Bible that was widely used in the Roman Catholic Church until the mid-twentieth century. Most of the translation was undertaken by Jerome, a Christian scholar (died AD 420). In the Roman Catholic Church the Vulgate is still the basis of the official text of the Scriptures.

Index

Acknowledgments

Alamy: p. 19 Classic Image; pp. 45tr, 62-63, 66br, 74, 114, 115, 119, 124 Lebrecht Music and Arts Photo Library; p. 54 Photos 12; pp. 67, 77 World History Archive; p. 69 Mary Evans Picture Library; p. 71 Bildarchiv Monheim GmbH; p. 72 North Wind Picture Archives; p. 75 ASP Religion; p. 76 19h era; p. 78br The Art Gallery Collection; p. 85 Historical Art Collection (HAC); p. 86tr PhotoStock-Israel; pp. 90-91 Eddie Gerald; p. 123 The Print Collector; p. 142tr Jon Arnold Images Ltd; p. 147 Sonia Halliday Photographs; p. 157 WILDLIFE GmbH; p. 162 World Religions Photo Library

Art Archive: p. 50 Cenacolo Santa Apollonia Florence/ Gianni Dagli Orti; p. 64 Private Collection/ Gianni Dagli Orti; p. 68tl National Museum of Art Mexico/ Gianni Dagli Orti; p. 152 Gianni Dagli Orti

Bridgeman Art Library: p. 39 Look and Learn

Corbis: p. 3; pp. 9, 84tr, 93 Pascal Deloche/ Godong; p. 12, 94, 133, 175 Brooklyn Museum; pp. 13tr, 17, 29tr, 130, 156, 165 The Gallery Collection; p. 16 Charles & Josette Lenars; pp. 22, 24, 25 Gianni Dagli Orti; p. 29r Paul C. Pet; pp. 32, 131 Gregor Schuster; p. 33 Philippe Lissac/ Godong; p. 34tr Ron Nickel/ Design Pics; p. 34bl Sandro Vannini; p. 36 background Dr. John C. Trever, Ph. D.; pp. 36bl, 42, 45tl, 49 Bettmann; p. 51 Geoffrey Clements; p. 52 background M. Angelo; p. 57 Gavin Hellier/ Robert Harding World Imagery; p. 58 Todd Gipstein; pp. 59, 117bl and background Fred de Noyelle/ Godong; p. 60 Steve Estvanik; p. 66tl Bojan Brecelj; p. 73 David H. Wells; pp. 78bl, 101 Dean Conger; p. 84tr Hoberman Collection; p. 87tl Claudia Kunin; pp. 92, 135 Richard T. Nowitz; p. 100. Araldo de Luca; p. 110 The Art Archive; p. 113 Angelo Hornak; p. 116 Chris Hellier; p. 120tl and background Jane Sweeney/JAI; p. 127 Ruggero Vanni; pp. 139, 145 tr Jon Arnold/JAI; p. 140 Arctic-Images; p. 141tr Shai Ginott; p. 141m, 142b Hanan Isachar; p. 142tm Francis G. Mayer; p. 144 Stephanie Colasanti; p. 146 David Lees; p. 148 Frédéric Soltan/Sygma; p. 149 Bob Krist; p. 150 Quentin Bargate/LOOP IMAGES/Loop Images; p. 151 Jim Hollander/ epa; p. 155 Kristy-Anne Glubish/Design Pics; p. 155mr P Deliss/Godong; p. 167tl Gideon Mendel

Getty Images: pp. 83, 166, 167tr, 169; p. 26 Paul Chesley; p. 37 Mesopotamian; p. 47 Egyptian; p. 87tr Time & Life Pictures; p. 95 Paul Piebinga; p. 96 Foto World; p. 97 Miguel Carminati; p. 103 The Bridgeman Art Library; p. 122 Dorling Kindersley

Lebrecht Music & Arts: p. 38

Lion Hudson: p. 52

Photolibrary: p. 14 Eyal Bartov; p. 48 Ivan Vdovin; p. 70 The Print Collector; p. 80 CM Dixon; pp. 99, 117mr E&E Image Library; p. 109 English Heritage; p. 132 Harald WENZEL-ORF

Scala: p. 20 Florence - courtesy of the Ministero Beni e Att. Culturali; pp. 21, 46 Florence

Topfoto: p. 41 UPPA; pp. 68bl, 112 The Granger Collection

Zev Radovan: pp. 11, 13bl, 15, 52tr, 141tl

Map Acknowledgements

Richard Watts Total Media Services: pp. 27, 28, 29, 31,60, 65, 86, 89, 104, 129,136, 143, 145

Lion Hudson

Commissioning editor: Kate Kirkpatrick
Project editor: Miranda Powell
Designer: Jo Laycock
Picture researcher: Jenny Ward
Production manager: Kylie Ord